Education in Ancient and Medieval India

EDUCATION IN ANCIENT AND MEDIEVAL INDIA

JAGDISH CHAND
Former Deputy Director of Education and
Executive Director of the Delhi Bureau of Textbooks,
Delhi Administration

ANSHAH

Anshah Publishing House

(2009, First Published in 2007)

Rs. 750

ISBN: 978-81-8364-019-0

2014 Impression

Education in Ancient and Medieval India

Published by:

ANSHAH PUBLISHING HOUSE
LG 18-19, Pankaj Central Market,
Patparganj, Delhi 110092, Ph.: 011-47322068
Email: info@shiprapublication.com
Website: www.shiprapublication.com

Contents

Preface

The book Development of Education System in India, published in 2004, provides comprehensive description and analysis of the development of education system from Vedic times to modern times. As per the requirement of market and demand of curriculum prescribed in various universities, the book covering a particular period is brought out independently for the benefit of students and educators. It is hoped that this volume Education in Ancient and Medieval India will be welcomed and its advantage also taken by the pre-service and in service teachers.

The volume derives its material from several original and secondary sources and the author is grateful to all the authors and their publishers.

Jagdish Chand

1

Education System in the Vedic Period

INTRODUCTION : RICH EDUCATIONAL HERITAGE OF INDIA

The most important contribution of ancient India not only for India but also for the world is in the field of education. It may also be remembered that education is not an abstract term. It is manifested in the cultural, economic, individual, philosophical, scientific, social and spiritual advancement. In other words, education is the means for developing the mind for the betterment of the individual and society. Seen from this perspective, the following views of great scholars and thinkers deserve mention.

Max Muller, the great German ideologist and scholar has paid the following tribute to the rich intellectual heritage of India, "If I were asked under what sky the human mind has most fully developed some of its choicest gifts, has most deeply pondered over the greatest problems of life, and has found solutions of some of them which well deserve the attention of even those who have studied Plato and Kant, I should point to India. And if I were to ask myself from what literature we here in Europe who have been nurtured almost exclusively on the thoughts of Greeks and Romans, and of one Semitic race, the Jewish, may draw the corrective which is most wanted in order to make our inner life more perfect, more comprehensive, more universal, in fact more truly human a life, not for the life only, but a transfigured and eternal life—again I should point to

India." ('Collected works of Max Muller, Vol. XIII, India What Can it Teach Us')

Albert Einstein—"We owe a lot to the Indians who taught us how to count, without which no worthwhile scientific discovery could have been made."

Arnold Toynbee, an English historian—It is already becoming clear that a chapter which had a Western beginning will have an Indian ending. At this supremely dangerous moment in human history (Nuclear Age) the only way of salvation for mankind is the Indian way.

Mark Twain, an American writer—"India is the cradle of the human race. Most valuable and the most instructive materials in the history of man are treasured up in India only".

P. Johnstone, An American Scientist—"Gravitation was known to the Hindus (Indians) before the birth of Newton. The system of blood circulation was discovered by them centuries before."

Will Durant, a scholar and writer—"India will teach us the tolerance and gentleness of human mind, understanding spirit and a unifying, pacifying love for human being. India is the motherland of our race and Sanskrit is the mother of Indo-European languages. She is the mother of our philosophy of mathematics, mother of ideals embodied in Christianity and mother of our democracy. Mother India is in many ways the mother of us all."

Emmelin Plunert, a great scholar, in her book *Calendars and Constellation*—There were very advanced Hindu astronomers in 600 B.C."

Lancelot Hogen, in his publication *Mathematics for the millions*—"There has been no more revolutionary contribution than the one which the Hindus made when they invented zero."

Hu Shih, a former Chinese Ambassador to USA—"India

conquered and dominated China for several centuries without ever having to send a single soldier across its border." (*Bhavan Journal*, May 15, 1999)

Dr. F.W. Thomas, "Education is no exotic in India. There is no country where the love of learning had so early an origin or has exercised so lasting and powerful an influence."

Abbe Raynall, a zealous 'crusader' visited Hindustan in the midst of the 18th century and observed, "When we attentively examine the accounts given by the travellers of the manners of the natives of India, we seem to wander among the ruins, the remains of an immense fabric. The original form is lost, but enough is preserved to convince us of the magnificence and regularity of the plans. Amidst a variety of absurd superstitions, puritive and extravagant customs, strange ceremonies and prejudices, we may discover the vestiges of sublime morality, deep philosophy, and refined policy; but when we attempt to trace the religious and civil institutions to their origin, we find that it is lost in the maze of antiquity. By the most ancient traditions, the Indians appear to have been first who received the rudiments of science, and the polish of civilisation. (*Philosophical and Political History of the Settlements in the East Indies*, A. Stratham and T. Cadell, London, 1798, Vol. I, pp. 39-40).

PERIODS OF ANCIENT INDIAN EDUCATION

Dr. Radha Kumud Mukerjee in his book *Ancient Indian Education : Brahmanical and Buddhist (1947)* divides the periods as Rig Vedic Education, Education in the other Vedas, Later Vedic Education, Education in the Sutra Literature, Education in the Time of Panini, Education in Kautilya's Arthshastra, Education in the Epics—all under Part I titled Brahmanical Education.

The second part deals with the Buddhist education.

SOURCES OF THE VEDIC AGE EDUCATION : VEDIC LITERATURE

No study of the source of Indian culture, education, philosophy and thought is complete without an adequate acquaintance and understanding of the 'Vedic literature'. The Vedic literature represents the most important and intrinsic part of life of the Indian people.

It is very essential to understand and appreciate our cultural heritage. Here an attempt is made to summarise the contents of the Vedic literature.

The Vedic literature consists of the following:

1. Four Vedas
2. Six Vedangas
3. Four Upvedas
4. Four Brahmanas
5. One hundred and eight Upanishads (11 are most important)
6. Six systems of Philosophy
7. Bhagwad Gita
8. Three Smritis

THE VEDAS

The Vedas are four in number : Rig, Yajur, Sama and Atharva.

The Vedas contain 20,358 verses.

The Rig Veda has the largest number of verses (10,522) followed by Atharva Veda (5,977), Yajur Veda (1,984) and Sama Veda (1,875).

The Rig Veda is the oldest among all the four Vedas.

The Atharva Veda mentions all the Vedas. It is also known as the 'Science of Medicine'.

The language of the Vedas is the ancient Sanskrit. The

language is of different styles—somewhere very complex and somewhere simple and easily understood.

The knowledge and wisdom of the Vedas is said to have been revealed by God to enlightened seers (*rishes*).

The Vedas have come down to us through an elaborate system of oral tradition. They were passed on from one generation to another through memorisation. The seers held that 'living by the teachings of the Vedas' was far more important than their memorisation and recitation.

The Vedas have always been held in high esteem and have specially influenced Indian way of life—its culture, history, literature, philosophy, religion, and science, etc. The contents of the Vedas may be categorised under the following three heads:

1. The '*jnana*' or knowledge and wisdom
2. The '*karma*' or actions or code of conduct
3. The '*upasana*' or dedication and devotion to God.

The Vedas have been translated in almost all the major languages of the world.

The Rig Veda—The Rig Veda is the most ancient of all the holy scriptures in the world. It belongs not only to the history of India but also of the world. It became the fountain head of the subsequent knowledge that followed. Its 1,028 hymns are divided into 10,522 verses. It is divided into books (mandalas) subdivided into 85 subsections. The number of verses varies from hymn to hymn. It incorporates a variety of subjects having important bearing on our daily life as householders, engaged in several professions, polity and religion etc.

The Yajur Veda—The Yajur Veda has 1,984 verses spread over forty chapters known as '*adhyayas*'. Twelfth chapter is the biggest one with 117 verses and thirty-ninth is the shortest with only 13 verses.

The Sama Veda—The Sama Veda or the Veda of the 'Holy Songs' ranks third in the usual order of enumeration of the Vedas but in sanctity it is next to the Rig Veda. It contains hymns of the devotion, taken mostly from the Rig Veda. It has 1,875 verses.

The Atharva Veda—The Atharva Veda is the collection of 5,977 verses spread over twenty books. Book XX contains the largest number of verses, i.e., 158 and Book XVII has only 103 verses. It primarily deals with medical sciences.

Principal Features of the Vedas

The principal features of the Vedas may be summarised as under:

1. The Vedas constitute the first source book of knowledge and wisdom.
2. The Vedas are for individual good, in the present life and future life.
3. The Vedas proclaim that the world is real and not a myth or an illusion.
4. The Vedas provide the primary source of an ethical code.
5. The Vedas have a message for all.
6. The Vedas stand for universal fraternity.
7. The Vedas speak of the eternal conflict that goes on in man even to-day—an internal conflict between truth and non-truth, between good and evil, between the baser and noble instincts, conflict between ignorance and knowledge and the ultimate victory of truth, victory of good, victory of knowledge and victory of light.
8. The Vedic philosophy is based on the glory of One God—Supreme Lord who is the 'Light' behind all lights and the 'Force' behind all forces.
9. The influence of the Vedas on human life is manifold.
10. The teachings of the Vedas are secular and are for

mankind, irrespective of caste, colour, creed etc.

11. The Vedas have a definite message for the guidance of human conduct in daily life.
12. The knowledge and wisdoms of the Vedas bring about realisation of truth, peace of mind and ultimate liberation.
13. The Vedic mantras evoke dynamic and psychic vibrations in the spiritual circle of our being and thus unfold the divinity.
14. The Vedas are a great repository of divinity.
15. The Vedas contain very noble ideas on goodness, uprightness and purity of life.
16. The Vedas accord the same status to women as to men.
17. The Vedas are not a thing of the past. They, though originated in the past, they illuminate the present and have a definite message for the modern man and guide towards a glorious and fruitful future.

Age of the Vedas

There is a great diversity of views regarding the age of the Vedas. No authentic date has yet been fixed as to when the Vedas were revealed. Again it is not known when they were definitely brought to the written form. Also it is equally difficult to say when they were edited and arranged under different heads and sub-heads. Nevertheless it is a wonder that they could be preserved and are available to us against all hazards of time.

B.G. Tilak puts the date of Rig Veda to be 4,000 B.C.

Jacobi has also put forth a date of Rig Veda to be 4,000 B.C.

Prof. Max Mueller assigns 1,200 to 1,500 B.C. to Rig Veda. However, he states that it is very difficult to give any definite date.

Dr. S. Radhakrishnan observes that the Vedic period is obscure—it may be 2,500 to 6,000 B.C.

According to Swami Dayanand, the Vedas have been existence since times immemorial.

The Vedas have been translated in several foreign languages notably English, French and German.

Interpretation of the Vedas

With a view to giving a correct interpretation and explanation of the Vedic words, one has to be familiar with Vedic diction, etymology, grammar and knowledge of several disciplines as numerous Vedic words have different meanings in different contexts.

SIGNIFICANCE OF THE VEDAS AS THE CHIEF SOURCE OF INFORMATION

The Vedic education derives its inspiration from the Vedas. The '*Rig Veda*' is considered as the first record of mankind and is usually accepted as the oldest book in the world. The knowledge and wisdom of the Vedas is said to have been revealed by God to the enlightened seers. Therefore the Vedas are also called '*Shrutis*' for the knowledge was acquired after 'hearing'.

Regarding the contents of the Vedas, there is a myth that they deal with hymns only to be recited at ceremonies and that they are of interest only to scholars engaged in unravelling the mysteries and the myths of the ritualistic past. However, even a cursory glance over the contents of the Vedas would reveal that their subject-matter is very comprehensive, absolutely related and essential to everyday life. The Vedas deal with every branch of knowledge and provide basic material of all arts and sciences. In fact they are the 'first source' of wisdom. They deal with every branch of human life. As observed by S.C. William Jones, "From the Vedas, we learn the practical art of surgery, medicine, music, archery and house building. They are an encyclopaedia of every aspect of life—

culture, religion, science, mysticism, ethics, law, cosmology and meteorology". Regarding the contents of Scientific Values of the Vedas, as Mrs. Wheeler Willox has observed "The most remarkable work containing not only religious ideas in perfect life but also facts which all sciences have since proved true. Electricity, radium, electronics, airships, all seem to be known to the seers who found the Vedas". This indicates the variety of the subjects taught in higher educational institutions during the Vedic period.

PHILOSOPHY OF LIFE IN THE VEDIC AGE AND EDUCATION

Philosophy to the Indian seer was a practical aid that showed the right way of living. It determined the ideals and ways of life. For having an adequate understanding of the main stream of Indian philosophy, it would be very relevant to explain important concepts like *'Purushartha'*, *'Dharma'*, *'Moksha'*, *'Vairagya'* and *'Nishkam Karma'* as these had great bearing on life and education.

'Purushartha' is a value or action which an individual seeks or does for the realisation of his desire or an end. The four *'purusharthas* in a graded order are 'artha' (wealth), *'kama'* (pleasure), *'dharma'* (righteousness) and *'moksha'* (spiritual salvation, freedom or liberation).

'Artha' (wealth or material things) is only helpful as a means of satisfying one or the other desire of human life.

'Kama' includes physical as well as psychological satisfaction of the natural urges of an individual wealth or money is valuable only to the extent it serves as a means to acquire goods and services.

'Artha', thus is an instrument value for the realisation of *'Karma'*.

'Dharma' is not only a central concept in Indian philosophy but also a unique one. It determines what we should do in

different situations. In fact it is an instrument of regulating life.

'Dharma' denotes right action or conduct. It has ethical and social values. It includes values like control of senses, honesty, non-injury, self-restraint etc. It puts a check on *'adharma'* (vice).

'Dharma' interpreted in the social context of the Hindu society is an ideal system consisting of four *'ashrams* (stages of life). *'Brahmacharya'* is the period of celibacy and of education; *'Grahastha'*, the life of the household; *'Vanaprastha'*, retreat from worldly bonds and, the *'Sannysa'*, the life of a hermit.

'Moksha'. This concept sums up the ultimate aim of life in Indian philosophy. It is self-realisation. It is becoming one with him. It is the state of spiritual bliss. It is freedom from the cycles of births and deaths. It is the loftiest end.

Philosophers and seers have suggested different ways for the realisation of *'Moksha'*. Three of them are considered very important. One is the practice of *'Nishkam Karma'* (selfless action). The second is *'Dhyana'* (meditation) and the third is *'Japa'* (repetition of his name).

According to some thinkers *'Moksha'* can be realised only after death while others think it can be realised in this life. In any case, the emphasis is on noble deeds and purity.

Some critics tend to regard Indian philosophy as individualistic; indifferent to social welfare, negative and pessimistic and not for the wordly individual. They criticise that Indian philosophy expects us to be a 'sanyasi' (hermit). But there is absolutely no truth in this charge. It must be remembered that Indian philosophy does not ignore the immediate objective of life. It is very clear that the objective of self-realisation is to be realised in society following the duties enshrined in the four *'Ashramas'* of life and according to life action. However, wealth through action must be learnt by following the righteous way of life, i.e., honesty etc. In fact Indian philosophy is very definite and specific. Each stage of life involves duties and values. Of course it is very liberal. It allows a lot of freedom to follow different paths to achieve salvation.

The primary concern of Indian philosophy is *'sarvajana sukhino bhavanti''* (Happiness for all mankind). What is recommended is not 'renunciation' of the world but 'self-renunciation'. 'Unselfishness' or 'selflessness' is the central theme of Indian philosophy.

In accordance with the above mentioned thesis, ancient Indian education system included two types of education, namely, *'paravidya'* relating to ecclesiastical or spiritual knowledge and *'apravidya'* concerning wordly affairs. Right approach to two types of education would ultimately lead to *'moksha'* or liberation.

The ultimate objective of life and education is summed up in the following ancient prayer,

असमतोमा सद् गमय।
तमसो मा ज्योतिर्गमय।
मृत्योर्मा अमृतं गमय।

Lead me from falsehood to truth!
Lead me from darkness to light!
Lead me from death to immortality!

The idea of truth, light and immortality constituted a triune unity, each subsisting in the other.

The entire educational process, i.e., the contents, the methodology and the role of the teacher were directed to the realisation of this sublime end.

SIGNIFICANCE OF EDUCATION IN ANCIENT INDIA AND ULTIMATE OBJECTIVE

Ancient educators and seers considered knowledge as the third eye of man which gives him insight into all worldly and non-worldly matters. According to them nothing gives us such an infallible insight as '*Vidya*' in the material as well as spiritual sphere. As already stated it leads us to our salvation, in the mundane sphere, it leads us to all-round progress and prosperity. The illumination and light given to us by '*Vidya*' shatters illusion, removes darkness and enables us to realise the true value of life. A person who does not possess the light of education may be really described as 'blind'. The correct insight which men and women get from '*Vidya*' increases their intelligence, efficiency and power.

Ancient Indians have emphatically averred that intellect as developed and refined by "*Vidya*' is the real power in the world. The benefits of '*Vidya*' are too diverse to be enumerated comprehensively. It nourishes us like the mother, directs us to the proper path like the father; and gives us delight and comfort like the wife. It increases our fame and makes us cultured and pure. When we are in the solitude of a journey, or of a foreign country, it serves as a valued companion. It is, thus a veritable desire-yielding tree '*Kalp Vriksh*'.

As the common saying in India goes:

Swadesh pujyate raja
Vidvan sarvatra pujyate.

A king is respected in his own Kingdom while a learned man is worshipped everywhere. The Hindu law-givers even go further and lay down that the very sight of a learned man is sacred.

Following material (verses) from the Vedas throw sufficient light on the objectives and practices of education.

O Lord! Illuminate the learner or the student for a higher and happy life. (A.V., VII. 6.1)

Learning and acquisition of wealth are two important objectives by which a successful life can be led. (A.V., VII. 68.3)

Knowledge or learning makes one humble, free of ego. This

humility leads to proficiency and by proficiency one earns wealth and by wealth one makes one's life happy and successful. (A.V., VI. 41)

The Brahmachari makes the earth and heaven more and more useful for himself and for humanity. He leads an austere and disciplined life. (A.V., XI. 5.1)

Practical Application of Learning

The teacher after imparting the knowledge and wisdom to the students directs them for the practical application so that they make use of this knowledge in various pursuits. (XV.XX. 12)

MAIN FEATURES OF THE VEDIC EDUCATION

1. *Free Education in Ancient India – A Philanthropic Mission*: In ancient India teaching was considered to be a holy duty which a Brahmana was bound to discharge irrespective of the consideration of the fee. Teachers were expected to devote their lives to the cause of teaching in the missionary spirit of self-sacrifice, and the society laid down the principle that both the public and the state should help the learned teachers and educational institutions very liberally. Fee was a minor item in the income of a private teacher and did not figure at all in the budgets of educational institutions including universities in ancient India. Society realised that '*Vidyadana*' or the gift in the cause of education was to be the best of gifts, possessing a higher religious merit than even the gift of land. Religion had a great hold over the public mind in ancient times. Society was always anxious to help the cause of free education to all in a variety of ways. On the occasion of religious feasts, students and teachers were invited and donations were given liberally. There were free feeding houses for the

poor in general and the students in particular. Well-to-do persons were expected to pay the maximum they could to the teachers.

2. *No State Control on Education*: Rulers of the country had very little directly to do with education. It was a private affair of the people, managed entirely by Brahmanas. Rulers of the country could subsidise it, if they thought fit to do so, with grants of land or money, but could impose no conditions or control on teachers affecting their freedom of work.
3. *High Status of Teachers*: Teachers were a highly honoured class—honoured even by kings. Kings rose from their thrones to receive great teachers such as Narada, Vashishtha and Vishwamitra. A well-known Sanskrit verse goes so far as to say:

   The teacher is Brahma. The teacher is Vishnu. The teacher is the Great God Shiva. The teacher is the Great Brahman (Supreme Divine Soul) incarnate. Bow to that teacher!
4. *Teacher as Parents*: Teachers behaved as parents to their pupils and pupils behaved as members of the teachers' family. The attitude of the pupil was to be one of complete submission.
5. *Residential Schools*: Teachers and pupils lived together and so identified themselves with one another. They prayed as follows:

   "May both of us be guarded! May both of us be protected! May both of us work together! May the study of both of us be successful (vibrant with power, radiant with light)! May we not be rivals to each other! Om, Peace, Peace, Peace".
6. *Immediate Aim – Vocational*: The immediate aim of education, however, was to prepare the different castes of people for their actual needs of life.
7. *Curriculum*: The subjects of instruction varied according to the vocational needs of the different castes from the

Vedas and Vedangas in the case of Brahmanas, to the art of warfare in the case of Kshatriyas, and to agriculture and trade, arts and crafts in the case of Vaishyas.

8. *Methods of Instruction*: The methods of instruction generally consisted of recitation by the teacher and repetition by the pupil, followed by explanation by the teacher, questioning by the pupil, and discussion between the teacher and the pupil.
9. *Individual Teaching*: Pupils were taught, individually, not *en masse* by the class method.
10. *Method of Study*: The method of study consisted in listening to the teacher, reflection on what has been listened to and its constant revision and discussion.
11. *Role of Travel in Education*: Travel was regarded as necessary to give a finishing touch to education.
12. *Education – Moral, Religious and Spiritual*: Education was not for a public examination or for paid public or private service, as it is generally considered to be at present. It was not merely intellectual. It was also moral, religious and spiritual.
13. *Forests as Centres of Education*: The place of education was generally the forest "far from the madding crowd's ignoble strife".
14. *Sanskrit as the Medium of Instruction*: The medium of instruction was Sanskrit.
15. *Self-Control and Self-Discipline*: Self-control or self-discipline was considered to be the best discipline. However corporal punishment was not altogether ruled out.
16. *Wide-Spread Education of Women*: In the earlier Vedic, and Upanishad times, girls were free to go through the '*Upanayana*' ceremony, live a life of celibacy, studied Vedas, Vedangas and other subjects along with their brother pupils.

17. *Science Education in Ancient India*: Vedic science included astronomy, mathematics, chemistry and biology. The Atharva Veda is known as 'the Science of Medicine'.
18. *Commercial Education in Ancient India*: Knowledge of commercial geography, needs of the people of various localities, exchange value and quality of articles, and languages spoken at different trade centres were considered necessary. Theory of banking was also included in the course. In the hereditary training families of high status, such a wide training might have been possible, but generally the knowledge about commerce and trade was picked up by working in the family shops or trades. There were no organised educational institutions, though most of the trades had formed efficient guilds during the first millennium of the Christian era. Training was usually imparted in the family by the elders in real learning situations.
19. *Mathematics Education in Ancient India*: Ancient India quite early evolved simple system of geometry urged by the necessity of accurately laying the open-air sacrificial places. *Shulvasutra* are the oldest mathematical works, probably composed between 400 B.C. and 200 A.D. Aryabhata (476-52) is the first great name in Indian mathematics. To the period immediately preceding him belongs one of the most significant of human discoveries, the zero, though the name of the discoverer is unknown.
20. *Ultimate Aim of Education – Self-Realisation*: The ultimate aim of education in ancient India was not knowledge as preparation of life in this world or for life beyond, but for complete realisation of self – for liberation of the soul from fetters of life, both present and future. That knowledge was real, which led to emancipation – led from unreality to reality, from darkness to light, from death to immortality.

AIMS, IDEALS AND OBJECTIVES OF VEDIC EDUCATION

Aims, ideals and objectives of education are always with relation to the ideals of society. While discussing this aspect, we may keep in mind that modern terms like democracy, secular, social communism, socialism, autocracy etc. were not in use during the Vedic age. Therefore, aims and objectives of education should not be discussed in the context of these terms.

Following were the main objectives of education:

1. *Ultimate Objective as Moksha (Liberation) or Self-Realisation*: Ancient Indians believed that education should prepare an individual in such a way as to prepare him to attain the objective of liberation, i.e., to be one with the Almighty and to be free from the cycle of births and deaths.
2. *Infusion of Piety and Religiousness*: In ancient India religion played a prominent part. Education aimed at the infusion of piety and religiousness in the minds of the pupils. Following methods were used for the infusion of piety:—
   (a) A student had to observe *'Vratas'* (religious observations) during his educational course.
   (b) He had to offer daily morning and evening prayers.
   (c) Religious festivals were celebrated every month in the Ashram or in the teacher's home. Thus a spiritual background was provided so that a student may withstand the temptations of life.

   But it does not mean that the renunciation of the world was encouraged. Leaving a few who were to remain life long *'Brahmacharis'*, the vast majority were to become householders.
3. *Education for Worldliness – Vocational Aim*: Happiness in other world was given more stress than the happiness in this world. This world, according to them, was unreal and

full of fetters. The highest wisdom was a release from these fetters. Yet they did not forget this world. Preparation for living was also one of the most important aims of Education. All the rules of conduct and duties of daily life of different '*Varnas*' show that they wanted man to prepare for present life. One must be true to his Duty (*Dharma*).

4. *Character Formation*: Education must form character. Mere intellect was not of worth if the person was devoid of not much morality. Morality or the right behaviour was the highest '*Dharma*'.

   Education was regarded as a means of inculcating values such as strict obedience to elders, truthfulness, honesty and temperance. Good conduct was greatly emphasised. It was believed that through good conduct, man gains spiritual merit, wealth and beauty.

   Following methods were used to form character:

   (a) Lessons on morality were given orally by the teachers.
   (b) The very environment in which students lived was calculated to give a proper turn to their character.
   (c) As there was the '*Gurukula system*', students were directly under the supervision of their teacher who was to watch not only their academic attainment but their moral behaviour also.
   (d) In everyday life, students were made to follow the rules of etiquette and good manners towards their seniors, equals and juniors. The rules helped in the formation of character.
   (e) The rituals and daily prayers helped to form good moral habits.

5. *Development of All Round Personality*: Ancient Indians believed that personality should be developed through education. Personality was developed through the following methods:

(i) *Self-restraint*: Students were taught self-restraint which helped in the enrichment of their personality. Self-restraint meant simplicity in life and habits. Celibacy was impressed upon.

(ii) *Self-confidence*: From the very first day of education in the '*Upanayan*' ritual self-confidence was fostered in the minds of the students. They were impressed upon to perform their duties in the right earnest. This was envisaged to develop self-confidence in them. Self-reliance was considered as the mother of self-confidence and the Brahmanic educational system sought to develop it in various ways.

(iii) *Self-respect*: A feeling of self-respect was developed in the student. The student was made to feel that he was the torch-bearer of the culture of race. A well educated youth was to be honoured more than the king himself. Such an environment developed the student's self-respect.

(iv) *Discrimination and judgment*: Powers of discrimination and judgment were developed in students to enrich their personality. They specialised in logic, law, philosophy, poetry and literature. These subjects were full of controversies and the student had to understand both the sides from his own judgment and define his position in literary debates. Thus his critical faculty was developed.

6. *Stress on Social Duties*: A student was not to lead a self-centred life. He was to perform his duties as a son, as a husband, as a father and many other capacities conscientiously and efficiently in the society. His wealth was not for his own sake or for his family; he must be hospitable and charitable. All professions laid stress on civil responsibilities.

7. *Promotion of Social Efficiency and Welfare*: The promotion of social efficiency and welfare was an equally important aim of education. Education was not imparted simply for the sake of culture or for the purpose of developing mental powers but for the purpose of training every member of society in the profession which he was expected to follow. Society had accepted the theory of division of work which was later on governed by the principle of heredity. Each family trained its children in its own profession. The purpose was to make each individual socially efficient.
8. *Preservation and Promotion of Culture*: The preservation and promotion of national culture and heritage was also stressed. "The services of the whole community were conscripted for the purpose of the preservation of the Vedic literature. Every person had to learn at least a portion of his sacred literary heritage." A section of Brahmanas had to devote the whole of their life to the cause of learning, to commit the Vedas to memory in order to ensure preservation.

EDUCATION OF WOMEN

The Vedas give a very honourable and respectable status to women. They were eligible for higher education, for the study of the Vedas and the performance of administrative and other important jobs mostly performed by men even today.

Boys should go to the schools meant for boys and girls should go to the schools where there are women teachers. (Y.V., 11.59)

Just as dawn dispels the darkness and gives pleasure, so also the learned ladies should remove ignorance of the girls and broaden their outlook, and be a source of pleasure. (Y.V., 34.4)

O learned lady! All the life is dependent upon you because you impart education to all.
(R.V., II. 97.17)

The women should have opportunity to attain knowledge of the Vedas from all the four corners (A.V., XIV. 1.64)

Those maidens who study the Vedas with the observance of *'brahmacharya'* and have perfect self-control become the ornaments of the human race. (R.V.I., 79.1)

Women Scholars and Seers

The Rig Veda mentions the names of the following scholars and seers whose hymns are found in the Vedas.

1. Apala (viii, 91, 1-7)
2. Devajami
3. Ghosha (i, 117, 7)
4. Indrani
5. Jarita
6. Juhu, (x, 109)
7. Kadru (ii, 6, 8)
8. Lopamudra (i, 179, 1-6)
9. Paulomi
10. Romasha (i, 126.7)
11. Savitri
12. Sraddha-Kamayani (x, 1.51)
13. Sharanga
14. Urvashi (x.95)
15. Vagambhrini (x.125)
16. Vishvavara (v, 28, 3)
17. Yami (x.10)

The Sam Veda adds the following:

18. Akrishtabhagha

19. Gaupayana (ib., xxii, 4)
20. Nodha (Purvachchika, xiii, 1)
21. Sikatanivavari (Uttarchchika, 1, 4)

During the Vedic period, women sages were called 'Rishikas' and 'Brahmavadinis' who were the products of the educational discipline of 'Brahmacharya' for which women also were eligible. Rig Veda (V, 7, 9) refers to young maidens completing their education as 'Brahmacharinis' and then gaining husbands in whom they are merged like rivers in oceans. Rig Veda (III, 55, 16) mentions unmarried learned and young daughters who should be married to learned bridegrooms. Yajur Veda (viii, I) also states that a daughter who has completed her 'brahmacharya' should be married to one who is learned like her. Likewise, the Atharva Veda (xi. 6) mentions learned maidens.

Role of the Mother in Education

A mother should impart education to her children so as to broaden their horizon. At this stage good manners are to be taught so that the children behave properly with the elders, and in assemblies. (R.V., V. 47.6)

TEACHER AS SPIRITUAL AS WELL AS INTELLECTUAL GUIDE

The teacher occupied a pivotal position in the Vedic system of education. The teacher was a parent surrogate (parent substitute), facilitator of learning, exemplar and inspirer, confident, detector friend and philosopher, moral educator, reformer, evaluator, character and personality builder, imparter of knowledge and wisdom and above all a guru, religious and spiritual guide.

The importance, which in modern times, is attached to the institution or the 'Alma Matter' was in ancient days attached to the teacher. The person who took charge of immature children and made them worthy and useful citizens in society was naturally held in high reverence. It was the function of the teacher to lead the student from the darkness of ignorance to the light of knowledge. The lamp of learning is concealed under a cover, says one educationist, the teacher removes it and lets out the light.

The relationship between the teacher and pupil was regarded as filial in character. Teacher was the spiritual father of his pupils. In addition to imparting intellectual knowledge to them, he was also morally responsible. He was always to keep a guard over the conduct of his pupils. He must let them know what to cultivate and what to avoid. He must instruct them as how to sleep and as to what food they may take and what they may reject. He should advise them as to the people whose company they should keep and as to which of the villages and localities they should frequent. During the Vedic period learning was transmitted orally from one generation to another. Great importance was attached to the proper accent and pronounciation in the Vedic recitation and these could be correctly learnt only from the lips of a properly qualified teacher. The spiritual salvation, depended almost entirely upon the proper guidance of a competent teacher.

Books being rare, the student had to rely upon his teacher alone. A sympathetic teacher unreservedly placed at the disposal of his pupils the essence of all his experience. Therefore, he got the highest regard and respect from his students and the society.

The teacher did not demand any fee but also helped the poor students in getting food or clothing. When the students had returned home after their education, they were to call on their teacher frequently by bringing him some presents; it may be even a tooth stick. Teachers also used to return their visits. The teacher's visit was not without its benefit to the student; he used to utilise the occasion to ascertain how far the ex-student was keeping up his reading and studies and leading a life as required. The mutual contact between the teacher and the student thus continued even after the completion of education and was for mutual benefit.

Every morning and evening the pupil went round the village for alms and whatever was given to him, he handed over to his Guru. This service was not looked down upon in the society. He ate nothing except what his Guru gave him. He used to fetch water, to gather fuel for the alter, to sweep the ground round the hearth, and to wait on his Guru day and night. This looks like menial service interfering with the student's studies according to the modern ideas, but one must bear in mind the accompanying explanatory regulation that the teacher was never to utilise the labour of his pupil for his own selfish, household purposes. At the command of his teacher, he shall approach, although the teacher may not be visible and if he sees his teacher standing or sitting in a lower place or to be wind-ward, he shall rise and change his position. If his teacher is walking, he shall walk after him, informing him of the work which he is going to do and telling him what he has done.

He shall do what is serviceable to his teacher. He shall always occupy a coach or seat lower than that of his teacher. He shall preserve chastity. In this way the complete moral and intellectual development was the objective of this ancient pedagogy. In this the teacher occupied an exhalted position.

Reasons for not Maintaining the old Relations by the Teacher and his Pupils

1. *Increased Number of Students*: The number of students in the past was limited and students used to receive their education normally at the residence of their teacher. It was, therefore, very easy for the teacher to develop intimate relations with the children under his charge. But now the number of students has gone very high. Sometimes this number goes up to sixty in a class. Not to talk of developing intimate relations, it has now

become a formidable problem for the teacher even to remember the names of all the pupils.

2. *Day Schools Instead of Residential Institutions*: There used to be residential educational institutions in olden times. The school was a large family and the teacher was the head. The students resided there for twenty four hours and for many years. Therefore, intimate relations were natural. But in the modern day schools the students stay for five or six hours and that too only on working days. It is, therefore, not possible to develop close mutual relations in such a short period.
3. *Subject Teachers*: With the growth of knowledge specialisation has become a key factor in every aspect of education. Consequently now-a-days we have specialist teachers as subject teachers whereas formerly there used to be a single teacher for students and he educated them throughout their educational period. The subject teacher of today does not look to the integrated development of the whole child as he keeps his own subject in mind. Moreover he has to deal with many students in the particular subject. These conditions make it difficult for him to develop intimate relations with his pupils.
4. *Missionary Zeal*: In the Vedic period, a teacher was selfless and he did not work for remuneration. Teachers were missionaries. Therefore, they worked wholeheartedly. Society was responsible for the fulfilment of their needs. But the teacher of today is a professional worker. He is perhaps more interested in his remuneration than his pupils.
5. *Materialistic Influence*: The West has infected India with materialistic attitudes. A teacher of materialistic attitude cannot be interested in his pupils as much as he can be expected to be in his material returns. This attitude affects his relations with his pupils also.

6. *Better Status of Teacher in Society*: The teacher of ancient India had a very high status in society. He was respected and honoured by society. Modern teachers do not enjoy such a high status. Therefore the pupil of today does not learn to show so much reverence to his teacher. Consequently the relationship between the two is not very intimate.

The Teacher in India by Prof. R.P. Singh describes the diminutive role of the teacher in these words : "The present-day teacher in India is a by-product of the emergence of the middle class in the latter half of the 19th century. In spite of some of the remnants of the glory of the past that are attached to his calling to this day, it is difficult to maintain that he is a direct linear descendant of his illustrious forbear ... Two major considerations as regards his diminutive role are: (a) The dignity of a teacher in the past, especially under Aryan rule, was not merely because of his learning but also because of his high caste; and (b) Teaching was an inalienable part of the priestly obligation monopolised by the Brahmin community, although technically speaking (until Manu) people from other communities could also become teachers..."

He further says, "The halo and power of a teacher of pre-printing days is gone. A teacher has diminishing teaching value; and in keeping kids busy elsewhere, he is a very helpful tool. Beyond that he has no power no control and therefore no status."

It is further observed, "The outstanding features of the teacher during the ancient and medieval periods, therefore, constituted his priestly character, restricted purpose, and an uneventful life in a more or less stable society. With the appearance of the British on the Indian scene in the early 17th century the Indian teacher, both Hindu and Muslim ... mullahs or pandits in their diminutive and considerably mutilated role, held their sway supreme at social functions but otherwise they could be conveniently forgotten."

The 'new' teacher according to Prof. Singh, who formed a segment of the newly created middle class by the British had "no mooring in the typical Indian soil. The major distinctions between the 'new' and 'old' profession lie (1) in their secular character, (2) in the systems of payments, and (3) in their outlook towards the jobs they do."

Prof. Singh draws a parallel between the situation in the United States and India and remarks, "... In the case of teachers in the urban centres of his country also the same dynamics of hire and sale is observable as it is in the case of certain other transactable commodities. The equilibrium of rural society is also being disturbed because similar strains of business are becoming, gradually, noticeable.

According to him, "the Indian teacher other than university teachers who regard themselves as a distinct group is almost the residual layer of the available intelligentsia."

"As a representative of the intellectual class also, his status has been appreciably eroded by the higher standards of proficiency required in other professions. Whereas the standard and variety of accomplishments now being expected in other walks of professional life have gradually risen, in teaching they have either remained stationery or slid down for want of challenge."

PROCESS OF INSTRUCTION

There were three steps in instruction: (1) *'Sravana'* (Listening), (2) *'Manana'* (Deliberation and reflection) and (3) *'Nididhyasana'*.

Sravana is listening to words texts as they are uttered by the teacher. It is the system of oral tradition by which India has built up its whole culture through the ages. Through this system, knowledge is conserved and transmitted from generation to generation. Thus the book of knowledge in those days was called *'Sruti'*, 'What was heard'.

'*Manana*' is the process of deliberation or reflection of the topic taught.

'*Nididhyasana*' represents the highest stage.

It is obvious that education in ancient India was not confined to mere learning by rote the sacred text books. The contemplation and comprehension of their meaning was considered as more important and vital to education than their mere mechanical recitation and correct pronunciation. There are several passages in the Rig Veda which condemn and ridicule those whose knowledge is confined only to the repletion of its words without insight into their inner meaning and emphasise the supreme need of realising the meaning by constant and concentrated contemplation. "He is only the bearer of a burden, the blockhead, who having studied the Veda does not understand its meaning, is like an ass, carrying a load of sandle-wood whose weight it feels without enjoying its fragrance". "Learning without understanding is called cramming, like dry wood on ashes, which can never blaze." The words of the Veda which are repeatedly recited as texts do not kindle and reveal their inner essence." The ideal of learning was the realisation of Truth and not the mere mastery or recitation of texts.

Method of Discussion and the Learned Assemblies

The highest stage of education was achieved through what was called as '*Brahmana-Sanghas*', the Assemblies of the learned or Academics where students of advanced learning got together for further advancement of knowledge by discussing their respective contribution to it.

Individualised Instruction

A modern teacher teaches students by 'classes' whereas a teacher in ancient India taught students as individuals. The pupil lived with his teacher as a member of his family. The school was the home of the teacher. It was a hermitage, amid sylvan surroundings. It functioned in solitude. The constant and intimate association between the teacher and taught was vital to education as conceived in this system. Education was student-centred and a student was the chief concern of this system of education.

ADMISSION AND EVALUATION SYSTEM

There seems to be no direct reference available to spell out the methodology followed by the Acharya to judge the adequacy of knowledge of his pupils. However, from the study of various hymns some inference could be made. Yaska and Sayana, famous commentators on the Vedas, have inferred from the Rig Veda hymn (X. 71.7) that the students were given three grades as under:

1. *Maha Prazanan* grade—students of high ability
2. *Madhyama Prazanan* grade— students of high ability
3. *Alpa Prazanan* grade—students of low ability

S. Narain in his book *Examinations in Ancient India* (1993) explains the system in these words, "These grades were given to the students as a result of their continuous assessment by their teacher. The system can be well compared with that followed by various examining bodies now-a-days on the basis of pedagogical research. Students placed in the highest grade, i.e., '*Maha Prazanan*' were only allowed to pursue the higher knowledge, while those of '*Madhyama Prazanan*' grade, i.e., medium ability were expected to be settled in their occupations, i.e., ploughing, etc. However pupils evaluated as low ability students, i.e., '*Alpa Prazanan*' grade were to be weeded out, i.e., dismissed from studentship. This is further corroborated from '*Nirukta*' (i.I)."

Admission to '*Brahmana Sanghas*'—Learned assemblies were made on the basis of oral questions of searching nature. (Rig Veda X. 71.7 and 8)

F.A. Keay in *Ancient Indian Education* observes that this system compares favourably with that followed in the Middle Ages in Europe.

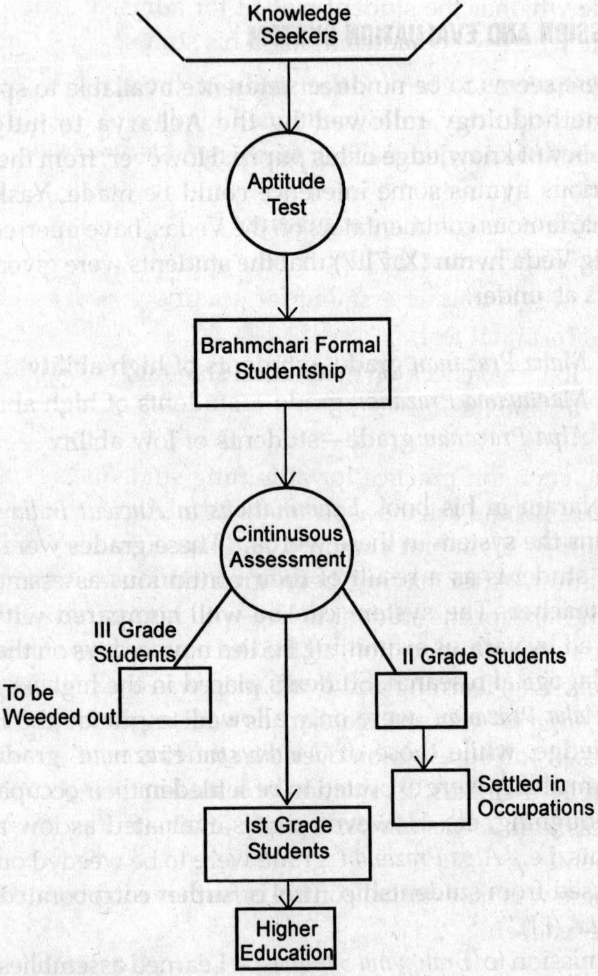

Fig. 1.1 : Admission and Assessment System in the Vedic Period, *Ancient India*, 1995.

AUTONOMY OF EDUCATIONAL INSTITUTIONS

Teachers in the Vedic period were autonomous in their work and they followed various methods of admission and assessment. A teacher was the sole pedagogic authority to decide whether the student was fit for admission and also to decide whether he had completed his studies.

According to Narain, the study of the ancient literature indicates that the under mentioned kinds of modes and tests were followed by the ancient teachers:

1. Screening test for admission.
2. Entrance test for higher education.
3. Continuous assessment for grading the students.
4. Terminal test.
5. External check on evaluation standard through learned assemblies.

The common practice for admitting students was that the '*Acharya*' would ask the aspirant for admission a few questions to adjudge his moral standard and sincerity to receive high education. After having been granted studentship it was compulsory for the student to live with his teacher. Under the Vedic system of education, all the three processes of education, i.e., teaching, learning and evaluation was entirely integrated. The '*Acharya*' was the teacher, as well as the evaluator and exercised full supervision over the students who were treated as family members. Evaluation of a student was a continuous process and it was almost a daily affair—in fact moment to moment.

There was no external control or supervision over the work of the teacher.

STUDENTSHIP

There is a long hymn in the 'Atharva Veda' (XI. 5) describing the ceremony pertaining to studentship. The initiation ceremony was called '*Upanayana*' (literally meaning leading near the teacher for instruction) which lasted three days. It laid down the foundation of a planned life. By '*Upanayana*', the teacher, "holding the pupil within him as a womb, impregnates him with his spirit and delivers him in a new birth". The pupil was then known as '*Dvija*' "born afresh" or "twice born". "What '*garbhadhana*' was to physical birth, the *upanayana* was to spiritual birth". The pupil owed his first birth – physical to his parents and the second birth spiritual to his teacher. The age for admission to studentship was usually between 5 to 8 years and was open to all '*Varnas*'. The rite of '*Upanayana*' was meant to purify body and mind and to make one fit for receiving education.

After '*Upanayana*' the pupil entered into a state of '*brahmacharya*' indicating that it was a mode of life, and a system of education. The '*brahmachari*' as the aspirant for education was now called lived according to prescribed regulations, i.e., physical discipline as well as spiritual discipline.

VOCATIONAL AND PROFESSIONAL EDUCATION

The Rig Vedic Society aimed at attaining material prosperity also. This is reflected not only in the nature of prayers but also in the active participation of the people in various economic activities, both agricultural and pastoral and to some extent commercial and industrial. The following prayers bear out this aspect:

O God, bestow me the privilege of enjoying the wealth earned by honest and hard labour. (R.V. VIII. 4.17)

A farmer should plough the field, sow the seeds, level the field and thereafter irrigate it at proper intervals. He should protect the field from all sides. He will thus have a good yield of Crop. (A.V. III. 17.4)

O God! Create among men who establish industries and enterprises by utilising all the resources available. (R.V.I. 31.8 and I. 116.3)

The Yajur Veda provides a list of 609 animals, their diseases and cases.

The Vedas also mention more than 100 medicinal herbs and plants.

There are several references in the Rig Veda which suggest that a sizeable population of society was engaged in various crafts and vocations. It is on account of the development and advancement of its various crafts, cottage type industries and agriculture that India was famous for its riches and wealth. Practising medicine was an important profession. A considerable part of the Atharva Veda is devoted to medical sciences. The teaching profession was highly honoured. The following hymns throw extensive light on the existence of some vocations. (R.V., IX. 12, 1 to 4)

1. We different men have different tastes and pursuits. The carpenter seeks something that is broken, the physician a patient, the priest someone who will perform sacrifice.
2. With dried-up faggots, with bird's feathers, with stones, the artisan continually seeks after a man with plenty of gold.
3. I am a poet, my father is a physician and my mother a grinder.
4. The daughter horse wishes for an easy-going chariot.

The following professions are mentioned in the Yajur Veda:

- Rearing Birds (Y.V. 24.21; 24.22 and 24.25)
- Experts in Aquatics (Y.V. 24.21)
- Rearing of Animals (Y.V. 16.25 and 25.31)
- Upkeep of Animal Health (Y.V. 25.32 and 38)

- Training of Animals (Y.V. 24.10, 25.29 and 42)
- Reference of architecture is found in the R.V. (V. 62.6)

The Rig Veda (IX-179) refers to an iron city and also a mansion with one thousand pillars which suggests that the craft of masonary later on developed into architecture. The Atharva Veda mentions the altars of different architectural shape to be constructed at different occasions.

From the Rig Veda (I. 110.3 and I. 111.1) it is concluded that training was given in the following disciplines of craft and technology:

1. Architecture,
2. Blacksmithy,
3. Boat making,
4. Carpentry,
5. Fort building,

6/7. Jewellery gold smithy,

8. Masonary,
9. Metal Work,
10. Ship building,
11. Weaving.

CURRICULUM

According to recent researches, following disciplines were included in the curriculum in the graded forms in accordance with the stages of education.

1. Anthropology.
2. Astronomy.
3. Economics.
4. Epistemology.
5. Eschatology.
6. Ethnology.

7. Geology.
8. Human Eugenies.
9. Husbandry and Veterinary.
10. Mathematics.
11. Military Science.
12. Nosology and Pharmacopoeia.

EVALUATION OF THE VEDIC SYSTEM OF EDUCATION

Merits of the Vedic System of Education

The system of education was well-organised. It was suited to the needs of the society. Education was considered as the greatest gift in ancient India. It was aimed at the development of the personality of an individual to its maximum extent. Education helped in the realisation of spiritual and moral values, besides preparing for worldly pursuits. It was freely available to all those who wanted. There was no system of paying fees as we find it to day. The relations between teachers and the pupils were based on love and affection. They were very cordial and intimate. Both were bound by mutual confidence and reverence. The relationship lasted for life. The teacher's status was very high.

Curriculum was quite comprehensive. Though mainly religious yet it provided for vocations also.

Evaluation was continuous as well as comprehensive. Education was a life long process.

Shortcomings of the Vedic System of Education

1. There was rigidity in instruction.
2. Discipline was very strict.
3. It did not adequately encourage self-expression of the pupils.
4. Instruction primarily depended on verbal instructions. It required repetition and encouraged rote learning.

5. Female education was not very widely prevalent though there were many women scholars of eminence.
6. System of education was dominated by religious considerations.

Altekar sums up the chief characteristics of the ancient Indian education system in these words: 'In the heyday of its glory, ancient Indian education was widely spread, women and a large section of the masses being admitted to its privileges. It was able to develop character and personality, to inculcate civic virtues, and turn citizens well qualified to follow their professions and discharge their duties in life. It was not only able to preserve the heritage of the past but also to enrich it from generation to generation. It produced a galaxy of able scholars and thinkers from age to age, who made important contributions to the advancement of knowledge in the spheres of philosophy, logic, mathematics, astronomy, medicine and chemistry. It enabled India to achieve high material prosperity by the excellent arrangements it made for training young men in arts, crafts and professions. The general principles which underlay the system, e.g., plain living and high thinking, the intellectual freedom, individual attention to students, the monitorial system, *gurukula* (hostel) system, location of the educational institutions away from the din and dust of city life, are sound and capable of giving good results even in modern times, if applied with due regard to changed circumstances.'

2

Later Vedic Education (1200 B.C. to 200 B.C.)

MAIN SOURCE OF EDUCATION DURING THE LATER VEDIC AGE

Following are the main sources which help us to know about the educational system during the Vedic Age:

1. The Vedangas
2. The Upvedas
3. The Brahmanas
4. The Upanishads
5. The Bhagwad Gita

Vedangas

With a view to pronounce and understand correctly the words contained in the Vedas, help books were needed. These help books are named as Vedangas. (Limbs of Vedas—'*angas*' mean limbs). They are six in number.

1. Shiksha (Science of Phonetics or Orthography)
2. Chhandas or Metres
3. Vyakarna or Grammar
4. Nirukta or Etymology
5. Jyotish or Astronomy
6. Kalpa or Practice

Upvedas

There are four Upvedas dealing with four subjects as under:

1. Ayurveda or Medicine
2. Dhanurveda or Military Science
3. Gandharvaveda or Music
4. Shilpa-Veda or Architecture and Arts

Brahmanas

Based on the Vedas, these books relate to everyday duties. Some of the unknown Brahmanas are:

1. Shatapath Brahman
2. Gopaltha Brahman
3. Aitareya Brahman
4. Sam Brahman

Shatapath Brahman is the most important. It is a voluminous prose work. It provides important information about the geography, history, philosophy and rituals etc. of ancient India. In fact it throws a good deal of light on almost all aspects of life and society of the period.

UPANISHADS

The word Upanishad means sitting devotedly. It brings to the mind the picture of an earnest disciple or learner learning from his spiritual guru or teacher. In the Vedic literature, the importance of the Upanishads is next to the Vedas. Apart from Indian scholars and seers, Europeans also have sung the glory of the Upanishads. In the words of Schopenhauer "In the whole words, there is no study so beneficial and elevating as that of the Upanishads. In has been the solace of my life. It will be the solace of my death." Prof. Max Mueller has observed, "If these words of Schopenhauer require endorsement, I shall willingly give it as the result of my own experience during my long life devoted to the study of...." Prince Dara Shikoh, son of Emperor Shah Jahan was so much impressed by the philosophy of the Upanishads that he translated these in Persian. In the introduction, he wrote, "I have studied many religious books but I got solace only from the Upanishads."

The Upanishads are the works of saints and seers. They mostly deal with matter, soul and God and their interrelationships. They try to answer the questions as to 'how' and 'why' the universe came into being.

According to the Upanishads, self-realisation comes through austerity, proper knowledge and truth. Inside the body, the self is full of light and purity and it is perceived by those who exercise self-control.

Traditionally the number of the Upanishads is given as one hundred and eight. However among them the following eleven Upanishads constitute the primary object of attention.

1. Isha Upanishad
2. Kenya Upanishad
3. Katha Upanishad
4. Prashna Upanishad
5. Mundaka Upanishad
6. Mandakya Upanishad
7. Chandogya Upanishad
8. Brihadaranyaka Upanishad
9. Aitareya Upanishad
10. Taitirya Upanishad
11. Shevetashvatara Upanishad

The Isha Upanishad embodies in its very opening verse the central theme of all the Upanishads, namely, the spiritual unity and solidarity of all existence.

The Kenya Upanishad illumines the nature of knowledge by pointing out the eternal knower behind all acts of knowledge and purifies man's concept of ultimate reality.

The Katha Upanishad holds a special fascination for its happy blend of charming poetry, deep mysticism and profound philosophy. Its charm is heightened by the two characters of its dialogue, namely, Yama, the teacher and Nachiketa, the student.

The Prashna, as its name implies is an Upanishad of questions. Each of its six chapters comprises a question asked by each of a group of six students on various aspects of Vedanta. The Mundaka, classifies all knowledge, into '*para*' (higher) and '*apara*' (lower).

The Mundaka, surveys the whole of experience through a study of the three states of waking, dream and dreamless sleep and reveals the '*Atman*', the rue self of man or the fourth state.

The Chandogya provides an impressive account of man's spiritual education and his growth from worldliness to spirituality.

The Brihadaranyaka, the largest of the Upanishads, as its name implies introduces to us four outstanding personalities who illuminate its pages. They are Janaka, the philosopher king, Yajnavalkya, the philosopher sage, Maitreyi, the deeply spiritual wife of Yajnavalkya and Gargi, the gifted woman speaker and philosopher. This Upanishad, through its fascinating dialogues conducted by these personalities expands the nature of the divinity of man and the spiritual solidarity of the whole universe in Brahman.

The Aitareya establishes the spiritual character of the Absolute through a discussion of the nature of the Self of man.

The Taittiriya provides a scientific definition of Brahman as "that from which all these human beings are born, by which, after being born, they live and into which they merge when they cease to be".

Life is Action. The second verse of Isha Upanishad states,

"In this world, one should desire to live one hundred years, but only by performing actions".

Six Systems of Philosophy

The six systems of philosophy deal with the causation of the genesis of the world, and they describe six causes of this creation.

1. *Naya System of Philosophy* (Logic) by Maharishi Gautam. It deals with mater.
2. *Sankhya System of Philosophy* (Psychology) by Maharishi Kapil. It is related to Atoms.
3. *Yoga System of Philosophy* (Aphorism) by Maharishi Patanjali. It is concerned with energy.
4. *Vaishekshika System of Philosophy* (Metaphysics) by Maharishi Kanada. It pertains to time.
5. *Mimansa System of Philosophy* (Through Determination of a Point) by Maharishi Jamini. It expounds Action.
6. *Vedanta System of Philosophy* (Theology) by Maharishi Vatsyana. It elucidates the concept of Supreme Being.

THE SMRITIS

The Smritis lay down the rule for the conduct of the human life. The seer Manu was the first law giver in the world.

The three Smritis are :

1. Manusmriti by seer Manu
2. Yajvaralkyasmriti by ser Yajavalkya
3. Parasharasmriti by seer Parashara

Manusmriti represents the character and spirit of Hinduism. It also forms to a considerable extent the foundation of Hindu Law of the modern courts. Though finally compiled between 200 B.C. and 200 A.D., it is based on much older materials. The work consists of about 2,700 verses. It is the earliest of the metrical law books.

THE BHAGWAD GITA

The Gita is so popular that it has more than 50 commentaries in Sanskrit and more than 250 commentaries in other Indian and foreign languages. Almost every year we find a new book on the meaning and message of Gita.

Various dates are ascribed to the Gita. B.C. Tilak, a great scholar puts the fourteenth century B.C. as the date.

Shri Aurobindo, the revolutionary turned philosopher and sage has stated the importance of Gita in these worlds "All we need of spiritual truth for the spiritual life is to be found in the Gita".

In size, the Gita is a little book of seven hundred verses. The verses are divided into eighteen chapters. It is in the form of a dialogue between Arjuna, a noted commander and Shri Krishna, an earthly manifestation of God—'*Avatara*'. The setting of the dialogue is highly dramatic. Arjuna is facing the huge army of his cousins with their supporters, many of whom are his elders including his 'guru' Dronacharya. Arjuna is to fight them for the enforcement of the claim of five Pandavas to their part of the ancestral kingdom which is not accepted by Duryodhana, leader of the Kaurvas. The sight of his dear ones dissolves his determination to fight and he lays down his arms and thinks of renouncing the world. Shri Krishna, who is acting as his charioteer urges him to fight for his right cause. Krishna succeeds in persuading Arjuna who ultimately wins the struggle.

The exposition of Arjuna's duty and exhortation to fulfil it constitute the theme of Gita.

Essence and Main Teachings of the Gita

The essence of the philosophy as contained in the Gita is

that with inner conviction, we should discharge our duties diligently and honestly, irrespective of the consequences and leave the rest to the Almighty. We must fight for justice and right cause.

Death is inevitable to one who is born. One who dies, he is bound to take birth. It does not, therefore, behave to grieve over an inevitable event.

Soul is immortal and the body is perishable. The cycle of creation is a hard fact from which, there is no escape.

The ordered progress of the world at large is so important that God takes on special forms of prophets of incarnations from time to time to ensure its progress by appropriate guidance.

To be content with personal perfection is a narrow ideal. The proper ideal is to give to the world the best and the utmost that one can and to take from it the least. The whole theme of the third chapter is the Philosophy of Action. This is also known as 'Karma-Yoga'—communication with God through action.

According to Gita, there are two ways of liberation—those of action and knowledge. However, the order of activity is more important. It combines personal good with social good.

The wise man acts as a source of guidance and inspiration to the ignorant masses.

The wonderful dialogue closes on the note of dedicated activity, promising glory, success and prosperity to the individual who combines physical valour, with divine wisdom and is entitled to *Moksha* or communication with God through liberating dedication.

Renunciation or '*Sanyasa*' is an attitude of the mind. It is not the cessation of obligatory activities but the dedication of those to God. One can be united with God if one transforms one's actions into Him. This is real renunciation.

Selected Verses from Bhagwad Gita

Soul is Immortal

As the dweller in the body experience childhood, youth and old age in the body, he also passes on to another body. The serene one is not affected thereby. (*Adhaya 2.13*)

The soul is neither born nor does it die. Coming into being and ceasing to be do not take place in it. Unborn, eternal, constant and ancient, it is not killed when the body is slain. (*Adhaya 2.20*)

As a man, casting off worn-out garments puts on new ones, so the soul, casting off worn-out bodies enters into the other that is new. (*Adhaya 2.22*)

Weapons do not cleave the soul, fire burns it not, water wets it not, wind dries it not. (*Adhaya 2.23*)

Death is Certain

Death is certain of that which is born, birth is certain of that which is dead. You should not lament over the inevitable. (*Adhaya 2.27*)

Action! Action! Action

Seek to perform your duty; but lay not claim to its fruits. Be you not the procurer of the fruits of karma; neither shall you lean towards inaction. (*Adhaya 2.47*)

Perform action, O Dhananjaya, being fixed in yoga, renouncing attachments and even-minded in success and failure, equilibrium verily yoga. (*Adhaya 2.48*)

Concentration of Mind

When also, like a tortoise its limbs, he can withdraw the senses from sense objects, his wisdom is then set firm. (*Adhaya 2.57*)

The excited senses, O son of Kunti, impetuously carry away the mind of even a wise man, striving for perfection. (*Adhaya 2.60*)

From anger proceeds delusion; from delusion confused memory; from confused memory the ruin of reason; due to the ruin of reason an individual perishes. (*Adhaya 2.63*)

Just as a gale pushes away a ship on the water, the mind that yields to the roving senses carries away his discrimination. (*Adhaya 2.67*)

EDUCATIONAL IMPLICATIONS

The greatest lesson for the learner is that he must have complete faith in his teacher who should also be devoted to his work. True knowledge, learning and wisdom are acquired through ceaseless action coupled with devotion. Concentration on studies leads to enlightenment and self-control. The main characteristics of the learner or a devotee are: He is a lover of knowledge and mankind. He is curious to know and has an abiding faith in his teacher. He very politely but with a subtle resolution puts questions to his teacher to solve his problems. The teacher also makes all possible efforts to enlighten his students and guides him in such a way as he attains the ideals of a self realised individual.

MAIN FEATURES OF THE SYSTEM OF EDUCATION

1. *Aims of Education*: Education should enable the realisation of true knowledge and achievement of Absolute. Education was considered as a process of inwardly meditation and thinking.
2. *Importance of Guru (Teacher)*: It was considered essential to sit at the feet of 'Guru' in order to gain 'Absolute knowledge'. Spiritual knowledge was considered so difficult and secret that it could not be achieved unless there was a well versed teacher to make it understood to the student.
3. *Duration of Study*: Though the course of study during this period had increased enormously yet the period of

study remained the same.

4. *Methods of Teaching*: Following were the three methods of teaching prevalent during the period:
   (a) *Sharavan* (Listening)
   (b) *Manan* (Meditation)
   (c) *Nididhyasan* (Realisation and Experience)

5. *Valedictory Function*: After completing education when the students were to leave Gurukul for their homes to enter life of a household, Guru gave them final instruction and advise in order to guide them in their future life. In the words of Dr. R.K. Mukerji, "These words read almost like Chancellor's convocation address of modern universities".

   "Always speak the truth, fulfil your duties, never ignore self-study. Do not break the ancestral and old tradition after giving 'Dakshina' to Acharya. Never leave Dharma. Do not miss the opportunity of becoming great. Never be careless in studying and teaching the Vedas. Don't be careless in duties towards gods and forefathers (Yajna and Shradha). Treat mother as goddess and father as god. Treat Acharya (Teacher) as god (Deva). Treat guest (Athithi) as god (Deva). Always perform deeds free from faults, whatever gift you give, give it with full regard and respect and with pleasure and humanity. Give with kindness.

   If any doubt arises in your mind regarding religion or good conduct, then take advice from the Brahmans, who are dispassionate, noble and kind hearted and fit for the purpose and follow as they do. This is my instruction to you, you follow it. You follow it in this very, form".

6. *Education of Various Castes*: Brahmans were mainly authorised for Vedic study and of spiritual knowledge but some Kshatriyas had also become great 'Rishis' and learned philosophers like Janak, etc.

7. *Education of Women*: Women were working even as teachers. They were trained in dancing, music, fine arts, etc.
8. *Daily Routine and Duty of Students*: Following duties were included:
   (i) *Practical*. This included,
      (a) *Bhikshatan* (Getting alms).
      (b) Keeping '*Yajnagni*, (Sacred fire) burning.
      (c) Taming the animals of the Ashram.
      (d) Cultivation.

   Getting alms cultivated modesty in the pupils, '*Yajnagni*' enlightened the spirituality of the mind and service of the animals and land, kept his health and character sound and pious.

   (ii) *Mental Education*. The main aim of mental education was self-study.

   (iii) *Moral Education*. This was related to the practice of good behaviour. The disciple had not only to lead the life of a 'Brahmachari' but also observe certain exercises to keep the purity of character. He had to take very simple and pious food. He had to keep his mind calm and peaceful. He had to put on simple clothes. Decoration of body was prohibited.

INSTITUTES OF LEARNING

A brief account of institutes or institutions of learning is given here.

1. *Vedic Schools : Centres of Practical Living*. R.K. Mookerji provides the following description, "Quite a network of Vedic schools was spread over the vast country, each of which specialised in particular texts of the Vedas and developed special commentaries of their own and later on even special codes of law so as to become a centre of

both life and learning. For in these seats of learning there was no divorce between theory and practice, thought and life, speculation and action ... It was education not merely in the contents of sacred love but also in the methods of living and self-culture according to ideals embodied therein".

Panini (4th century B.C.) mentions some 24 such schools of higher learning.

2. *Mobile Debates*. For pursuing higher studies a student would travel far and wide to come into contact with celebrated teachers and hold discussion with them.
3. *The 'Charakas' or Wandering Scholars*. There were scholars who moved throughout the country and also taught the wandering students from place to place in search of knowledge.
4. *Assemblies or Conferences*. Renowned thinkers were invited to exchange views and to discuss philosophical issues in the assemblies by the Kings.
5. *Seats of Sacrifice as Seats of Learning*. The sacrificial sessions which sometimes passed for as many as 100 days provided opportunities for learned discussions among the scholars. These also provided practical and functional knowledge.
6. *Kings' Courts as Centres of Learning*. Among the important courts which served as centres of learning, mention may be made of the following: (i) Court of King Janaka of Videha, (ii) Courts of the Kings of Kosala, (iii) Court of the King of Kekaya, (iv) Court of the King of Madras.
7. *Parishads*. The Parishads were the assemblies of the learned scholars and teachers. Sometimes students were also the members of these assemblies. These were different faculties represented by scholars. Some scholars regard these assemblies as settlements or places where learned people resided. Whatever, the nomenclature, discussions on important topics took place at these

assemblies. According to F.A. Keay, these were important centres where a number of students who were receiving instructions at different places gathered and participated in discussions. Thus these '*Parishads*' formed the nucleus of something corresponding to a university. The '*Parishads*' played an important role in the promotion of education.

8. *Agrahara Village*. On auspicious occasions, kings used to invite learned Brahmanas, settle them in villages and assign their revenues to them for their maintenance. Such villages were called Agrahara villages, and they naturally became centres of learning where higher education was imparted free in different branches of Sanskrit studies. We shall mention about one such Agrahara village which was typical of its class.
9. *Kadiyur Agrahara* : The village of Kadiyur, modern Kalas, in Dharwar district in Karnataka, was made an Agrahara village in the 10th century by the Rashtrakuta administration, and assigned to 200 Brahmanas, who were well versed in Vedas, grammar, Puranas, logic, works on polity, the science of literary composition and the art of writing commentaries. The village was famous as an efficient centre of education.

ELIGIBILITY FOR HIGHER EDUCATION

Higher education began after 12 years of schooling. Several methods were used to test the eligibility of the student for higher education. One of the most important components of the method was to ascertain the true quest of the aspirant for knowledge. Proper mental calibre of the aspirant was another factor. Sometimes 'temptation' was offered in lieu of knowledge. Long waiting before imparting instruction was also resorted to. Following throw some light on the numerous typical methods used for assessing the suitability of the aspirant for higher education.

Chhand Upanishad (IV-2) mentions a King Janasruti Pantrayana who approached a teacher named Raikna for instruction and offered him 600 cows, a necklace and a carriage of mules in lieu thereof. However, the latter rejected the offer as he did not find the King eligible for instruction.

Katha Upanishad points out the case of Upakosala Kamalayana who tended fire of a teacher named Satya Kama Jaliala for a period of 12 years but was found unfit for higher knowledge.

Katha Upanishad mentions an interesting example. Nachiketa approached Yama for instruction. Yama offered him several temptations like gold, elephants, horses, etc. for diverting him from higher studies but Nachiketa was least tempted and replied, "Keep thou thy horses—No man can be made happy by wealth". Yama had to yield and he admitted Nachiketa.

WOMEN'S EDUCATION

The available evidence shows that there were learned ladies and that they shared the intellectual pursuits like men. The Brihaḍaranyaka Upanishad (VI. 4, 17) mentions an interesting ritual by which a person prays for the birth to him of a daughter who should be a 'pandita' or a learned lady. The 'Kaushitaki Brahmana' (VII. 6) tells a story of a lady named Pathyasvasti going to the north for study and obtaining, the title of 'Saraswati' by her learning. Of the two wives of Yajnavalkya, one took an important part in the disputations on philosophical topics (Brihad III. 4, 1, IV. 5.1).

SANSKRIT AS THE MEDIUM OF INSTRUCTION

R.K. Mookerji observes that during the Brahmana period and down to later times, there is no doubt that as F.W. Thomas has pointed out (JR'AS., 1904), "Sanskrit was the language of public religious rites, of domestic ceremonies, of education, and of science".

TEACHER'S DUTIES AND QUALIFICATIONS

A teacher was expected to possess the highest moral and spiritual values says the '*Katha Upanishad*' (I.2.8), "This truth is not grasped when taught by an inferior person". The '*Mundaka*' (I.2.12) requires the teacher to be well-versed with the sacred core and dwelling entirely in the Brahman. Again the '*Mundaka Up.*' enjoins upon the teacher that when a fit pupil approaches him, he should teach him the truth exactly as he knows it (I. 2.13). The teacher should not conceal the truth for such concealment would spell ruin to him ('*Prasna*', VI. I). The '*Taittirya Aranyaka*' (VII.4) lays down that the teacher must teach with all his heart and soul. According to '*Satapatha Brahmana*' (I. 1.26, 27), the teacher is bound to reveal anything to this pupil.

The teacher, however, was quite free to impart the knowledge to his pupil for which he was fit for. (*Taitt.* III. 5.2.1)

Very often teachers were very anxious to get pupils from all quarters. A prayer is contained in the '*Taittiriya Upanishad*' (I. 4.3), "As water runs downward, as the months go to the year, so, O God, many Brahmacharinis always come to me from all quarters." This desire was natural in teachers who felt that the truths they had discovered should live after them in their pupils. At the same time good teachers themselves were sought after by many pupils. ('*Bri. Up.*', III. 3.1, 7.1)

STUDENTSHIP

The Upanishads required that the Brahmacharin (student) before he was taught the highest knowledge of the Brahman, should show that he was calm and unperturbed in mind ('*Katha.*' II. 24; '*Mund.*' I.13; '*Svet.*' VI. 22) self-restrained, self-denying ('*Kath.*' I); and patient and collected ('*Kath.*' I).

'*Aitareya Aranyaka*' gives the following important regulations which were to be followed by a student:

1. The student should sit on the ground.
2. The student should not lean backward while learning nor lean forward.
3. The student should not be covered with too much clothing.

CONVOCATION OR FAREWELL ADDRESS

At the end of his education, the student was presented to the learned assembly and the teacher exhorted the student with these words, "Speak the truth. Do your duty. Do not neglect the daily study of the Vedas. After having brought to your teacher his proper reward, do not cut off the thread of your race. Do not neglect what is useful. Do not miss opportunities to become great. Do not neglect the sacrificial rituals due to the gods. Let your mother be to you like a goddess. Let your father be to you like a god. Let your teacher be to you like a god. Let your guest be to you like a god. Whatever actions are blameless, these should be followed, not others. Whatever noble actions have been performed by us, these should be emulated by you, not others. Learned persons should be respected by giving them a seat. Whatever is given should be given with faith, with joy and humility. If there should be any doubt in your mind, with regard to any duty or with regard to conduct, in that case, conduct yourself with Brahmanas (learned person) who possess good judgment, conduct themselves therein, whether they be appointed or not as long as they are not too severe, but devoted to duty. Thus conduct yourself. This is the rule. This is the teaching. This is the true purport (Upanishad) of the Veda. This is the command. This you should observe." (*Tait. Up.* I. 11)

CURRICULUM: SUBJECTS OF STUDY

On the basis of references and in the Upanishads and other works, R.K. Mookerji lists the following subjects.

1. The Vedas
2. Anushasana including (a) Phonetics, (b) Ritualistic Knowledge, (c) Grammar, (d) Exegetics, (e) Metrics, (f) Astronomy.
3. Vidya – Philosophical systems of Nyaya, Mimamsa etc.
4. Vakvovakyam – Special theological discourses on spiritual matters.
5. Itihasa-Purana – Stories of old heroes and heroines, cosmological myths or accounts such as "In the beginning this universe was nothing but water", etc.
6. Akhayana – Stories relating to Ashvameda.
7. Anvakhyana – Supplementary narrative.
8. Anuvyakhyana – Explanation of mantras.
9. Vyakhyana – Commentary.
10. Gatha – Song or verse epitomising the sacrifice of famous Kings.
11. Brahmana – Religious explanation.
12. Kshatravidya – The science of the ruling class.
13. Rashi – Science of numbers or arithmetic.
14. Nakshatra Vidya – Astronomy. Science of the lunar mansion.
15. Bhuta Vidya – Science of creatures that trouble men and the means of warding them.
16. Sarpa Vidya – Science of snakes.
17. Daiva – The knowledge of portents.
18. Nidhi – The science of divination.
19. Pitrya – The science of rituals concerning the worship of manes.
20. Sutra – Rules for the guidance of sacrifices and so forth.
21. Upanishads.
22. Shlokas – Mantras found in the Brahmanas.
23. The Veda of Vedas – Grammar of old Sanskrit.
24. Ekayana – Science of conduct.

25. Deva Vidya—Science of worship of gods.
26. Brahma Vidya—Science of pronunciation, ceremonial science. Prosody.
27. Devagana Vidya—Interpreted differently—Art of making (i) perfumes, (ii) Dyeing, (iii) Dancing, (iv) Singing, (v) Playing on musical instruments, (vi) other fine arts, (vii) science of medicine.

In the *Chandogya Upanishad* (VII. 1), when Narada approaches Sanat Kumara with the request to teach him, Sanat Kumara asked him: "Please tell me (first) what have you studied thereafter, I shall tell you what is beyond". Narada said, "I have studied, most reverend Sir, the Rig Veda, the Yajur Veda, the Sam Veda, the Atharva Veda as the fourth; the fifth Vedas Epic and Mythological poems; grammar; the Pitrya (the rules for performing rites of the ancestors); the Rasi (science of numbers), the Daiva (science of portents); the Nidhi (Science of divination); the Vakevakya (logic); the Ekayana (ethics); the Dev Vidya (Etymology); the Brahma Vidya (Pronunciation, Siksha ceremonial, Kalpa, prosody, Chhandas); the Bhut Vidya (science of demons); the Kashatra Vidya (the science of rulers or weapons); the Nakshatra Vidya (Astronomy); the Sarpa and Devajana Vidya. (the science of snakes, various arts and sciences)". This indicates that the curriculum was broad based.

H.D. Sankalia (1934) lists the following subjects in the curriculum during the times of Panini (About 600 B.C.)

1. The Vedas.
2. Anusasana or the six Vedangas.
3. Vidya—Vishvavidya.
4. Vakovakyam—art of disputation.
5. Itihasa—Puranas.
6. Akhyana.
7. Anvakhyana.

8. Anuyakhyana—mantras.
9. Vyakhana.
10. Gatha.
11. Narasanisi.
12. Brahmana.
13. Ksatra Vidya.
14. Rasi Vidya.
15. Nakshtra Vidya.
16. Bhuta Vidya.
17. Sarpa Vidya.
18. Nidhi Vidya.
19. Atharvangivasa.
20. Daiva Vidya.
21. Pitrya Vidya.
22. Sutra—rules for sacrifices.
23. Vedanam Vedam (grammar of old Sanskrit).
24. Ekayan—Science of conduct.
25. Dev Vidya—Science of exegetics.
26. Deva Jnana Vidya—making of perfumes and various arts like dancing, singing, etc.

Note: It appears all the subjects were not compulsory. Probably students had some option in the selection of subjects.

PROCESS OF INSTRUCTION

In learning, the main role was to be played by the student himself. It is clearly mentioned in the '*Brihadaranyaka Upanishad*' that the best instruction depends upon the three processes following one another, viz., (1) '*Sravana*', (2) '*Manana*' and (3) '*Nididhyasana*'.

'*Sravana*' is listening to what is taught by the teacher. Listening depends upon (a) '*Upakarma*'—a formal ceremony to be performed before reading the Veda, (b) '*Abhyasa*'—constant practice or recitation of the text, (c) '*Apurvata*'—

immediate apprehension of the meaning, (d) *'Phala'* — comprehension of results, (e) *'Arthavada'* — study of explanatory texts, the 'Brahmana' texts and (f) *'Upapatti'* — attainment of conclusions.

'Manana' is defined as contact contemplation.

'Nididhyasana' — concentrated contemplation of the truth so as to realise it.

Questions and Answers Approach

The pupils asked questions and the teacher discussed these at length. (*'Prasana'* III. 27)

All the familiar devices of oral teaching such as illustration (*'Prasana'* II), stories (*'Katha'*) and parables (*'Kena'*) are found utilised. The *'Taittiriya Brahmana'* uses the technical terms *'Prasnin'* — questioner; *'Abhi-Prasnin'* (cross questioner) and *'Prasna-Viveka'* — answer.

Use of discussion and disputation was also made.

'YOGA'

'Yoga' owes its beginning to the Upanishads.

'Yoga' implies withdrawing the organs from the objects of sense and concentrating them on the inner self. This method is aimed at self-realisation. The system implies eight external practices:

(1) *'Yama'* — abstinence from doing injury, honesty, truthfulness, chastity;

(2) *'Niyama'* — self-restraint;

(3) *'Asanam'* — sitting in the right place and in the correct bodily posture;

(4) *'Pranayama'* — regulation of the breath;

(5) *'Pratyahara'* — suppression of the organs of sense;

(6) *'Dharana'* — concentration of attention;

(7) *'Dhyanam'* — meditation;

(8) '*Samadhi*' – absorption.

'*Yoga*' was developed into a formal system by Pantanjali.

UNIVERSAL EDUCATION

Asvapati Kaikeya, a learned and an ideal king proclaimed, "In my kingdom, there is no thief, no miser, no drunkard, no man without an altar in his house, no ignorant person." ('*Chhand Upanishad*' V. 11.5)

MOST PROMINENT SCHOLARS OF THE LATER VEDIC

Period Yajnavalkya (about 600 B.C.). He was the most learned teacher of his times, unparalleled in his knowledge of '*Brahman*'. In the distinguished assembly of scholars called by King Janaka, Yajnavalkya maintained his superiority over all the scholars like Asvala, Artabhaga, Gargi, Uddalaka and Vidagdha. In the end he asked if anyone or all of them would desire to question him or would desire him to question them, but no one dared to take up the challenge. He imparted the sacred knowledge of '*Brahman*' to King Janaka, his former teacher, who was so much moved that he offered his entire kingdom along with himself to the great scholar. He protested against the priest's demand of sharing the benefit of the sacrifice. His view was, "How can people have faith in this? Whatever be the blessing for which the priests pray, this blessing is for the worshipper alone". He was the author of '*Yajnavalkya Smriti*'.

Janaka. A Kshatriya King, he was a very learned scholar and honoured the scholarship of other learned men. His court adorned several scholars and was a renowned centre of Vedic culture and civilisation.

Gargi Vachaknavi. She was a lady of great scholarship and one of the most prominent philosophers of her time. She even questioned the superior knowledge of Yajnavalkya. At the end of the philosophical discussion Gargi admitted Yajnavalkya's superiority and announced Never shall anyone defeat him in any argument concerning 'Brahman'.

Panini (Between 4th and 7th century B.C.). He was a renowned poet and grammarian, he authored the noted '*Ashtadhyai*' (comprising eight chapters), the earliest standard Sanskrit grammar and authority still in use today. He is said to have authored eight other works of four chapters each. His works consist of 4,000 sutras or aphorisms, each of 2 or 3 words only, covering all the grammatical rules. The '*Ashtadhyai*', the earliest scientific grammar in the world, not only systematised the language but also influenced all subsequent Sanskrit language.

Little is known about the life of Panini. It is likely that he was born at Attock in the Gandhara region.

Kautilya (4th century B.C.). also known as Chanakya and Vishnugupta, the author of the '*Arthashastra*' he was the Prime Minister and the close adviser of King Chandragupta Maurya (324-298 B.C.). He is often compared with Machiavelli's '*Prince*' of the 16th century A.D. This indicates that India was 12 centuries ahead of the world as regards higher knowledge in political economy and statecraft. He is described as a very 'wise and revered teacher'. His is a treatise on statecraft. It is of great interest as a primary source on the theory and practice of political economy in ancient India, especially of the Maurya rulers. The tone of the work is pragmatic and worldly-wise throughout. The standard of the contents of the book indicates that at that time, subjects other than religion also received appropriate attention at the level of higher education. He is said to have studied and taught at the University of Taxila. This again speaks of the existence of institutions of higher learning in ancient India when most of the Europe was educationally very backward.

THE GURUKUL SYSTEM OF EDUCATION

Meaning of the Gurukul System of Education. It was a system of education in which the student resided with his teacher in his home and received education. The family of the teacher became the family of the student.

Gurukul System as an Important Aspect of Vedic System of Education

The Gurukul system which necessitated the stay of the student away from his home and at the house of a teacher was one of the most important features of ancient Indian education. Hindu '*sastras*' recommended that the student should live under the supervision of his teacher. Direct, personal and continuous contact with a teacher of noble character naturally had great impact on the scholar during the pliable period of childhood and adolescence. The close association with elderly students, scholars and the wise induced the students to emulate their examples.

The students lived under the roof of their preceptor and therefore they were called '*antevasin*', meaning one who stays close to his teacher, i.e., under his roof. The Chhandogya Upanishad describes the student as '*Acharya-kula-vasin*', i.e., one who dwells in the house of the Acharya. Thus, the usual system of education in ancient India was for the students to live in the house of his guru under the latter's personal supervision.

This Gurukul tradition is reflected in the Universities of Oxford and Cambridge to a certain extent.

Counter Protection of the Gurukul System

The Gurukul system was best fitted to contribute to formation of character, the building of the personality, the preservation of the ancient culture, and the training of the rising generation in the performance of their religious and social duties. The daily association between the teacher and the taught had many beneficial results. The teacher had the advantage of daily watching the intellectual progress and the moral behaviour of his pupil. The constant presence of the teacher contributed in a great measure a spirit in the pupil to cultivate a feeling of reverence for elders; so lacking at present. A deep and solid foundation was laid for a well-ordered and disciplined life. The daily routine of a pupil was marked by simplicity, endurance, a rigid adherence to rules of hygiene and *'brahmacharya'*, in pure surroundings free from all unhealthy influences, and thus assured a healthy and robust human personality.

Liberal Education: The Gurukul ideas was in every way suited for instilling all the attributes of what is considered a liberal education. As is justly claimed by the Oxford and Cambridge Universities, they sought to turn out each graduate a scholar and a gentleman, that is what was achieved by the ancient Gurukul system. There can, therefore, be no doubt that the system is a valuable contribution to any educational scheme.

Spiritual and Religious Education: The strongest point of the system of education in ancient India, particularly in Vedic times, was that it was religious as well as spiritual through and through. Education should not be sectarian. Education is not worth the name, if it is not religious. We cannot do better than support this point of view, with a quotation from the great philosopher and eminent educationist, A.N. Whitehead. He says, "The essence of education is that it is religious. What is religious education? A religious education is an education which inculcates duty and reverence. Duty arises from our potential control over the course of events. Where attainable knowledge could have changed the issue, ignorance has the guilt of vice. And the foundation of reverence is this perception, that the present holds within itself the complete sum of existence backwards and forwards, that whole amplitude of time which is eternity."

Present System: The present educational system in India is defective in certain vital respects. In the formative period of the lives of young ones, we can conceive of very little for the development of character, adoption of high moral standards and the expansion of the mind and intellect than the daily contact and association with a right teacher. Our educational system does not afford any such opportunity. The teacher and the taught are thrown together at certain stated periods of the school or college but this hardly enables the teacher to mould the minds of his pupils. Intellectual attainments alone are of not much value. As Carlyle puts it: "Without hands a man might eat and could still walk but consider it—without morality, intellect was impossible for him."

Many students who study in colleges are living away from their parents. They are thus neither under parental authority, nor under proper control of their teachers or professors. The result is that the rising generation is falling an easy prey to all sorts of unhealthy influences. The school or college curriculum has not been devised so as to give adequate attention to the glorious facts of Bharatiya culture, with the result that our young men are fast developing a feeling of scant respect, if not of scorn.

Some of these shortcomings of our present educational system can to a great extent, be remedied, if the Gurukul system is introduced for a few years at least, in the educational scheme, care being taken in the selection of right teachers.

"Far from the madding crowd," the Indian culture was born in the lap of serene and divine Nature. Surrounded by the vast natural life and multi-coloured deep forests, man began to discover harmony between his spirit and spirit of Universe. The forests and flowers, woods and pastures, brooks and springs, deep valleys and lofty mountains gave him spiritual message. To realise this proximity with Nature, the Gurukul system came into being."

SANSKARS (CEREMONIES OR RITUALS) ASSOCIATED WITH THE SYSTEM OF EDUCATION IN THE VEDIC PERIOD

In the Vedic age, as already stated, education was given an important place. At every stage of education, one or the other ceremony was performed to make the occasion an auspicious one. Here these ceremonies are described in brief.

1. '*Vidyaramba Sanskara*' or '*Akshar Swikaran Sanskar*': This ceremony marked the commencement of child's education. This stage may be compared with the modern pre-primary stage. In the midst of a magnificent congregation, this ceremony was performed. It took place when the child was five years old. '*Saraswati*' (The goddess of learning) was worshipped. The child was taught to write the letters of alphabets with a pen of silver or gold on a mound of rice spread on the floor. The child was put under the charge of the preceptor (teacher). This was the first ceremony in the educational case of the child.
2. '*Upanayana Ceremony*': The Upanayana ceremony was originally performed when a student commenced his Vedic education under the supervision of a teacher, with whom he usually lived. Usually this ceremony was performed when the child was between eight to twelve years of age. (There is great divergence of views regarding age). In medieval time also this ceremony was performed under the holy 'pipal' tree. Whenever a student went to a new teacher, this ritual was performed. The ceremony opened with a breakfast during which the boy had to share food with his mother in the same dish. Breakfast was followed by a shave. The boy was then given bath and offered a Kaupina (a small strip of cloth used by children to cover their private parts) or Dhoti. A girdle was tied round his waist as a support

for Kaupina. The verses recited on the occasion of tying the girdle informed the boy that his belt was daughter of faith and a sister of the sages, possessed the power of protecting his purity and chastity and would keep him away from evil. The boy was then asked to offer '*Smidha*' (a piece of sacred fuel) to the glowing fire and the verses recited on the occasion prayed that God Fire should be auspicious to the young scholar and endow him with brilliance, intelligence and vigour so that his scholarship should glow up like the flame. In order to intensify his piety, the boy was then presented to a number of Vedic deities like '*Savitri*' who was charged with the special duty of protecting the student from harm, disease and death. The teacher then assured his pupil that he was henceforth under Divine protection. Then followed the actual initiation of the student in Vedic studies which was done by teaching him a prayer to the Sun (*Savitri Mantra*) also called '*Gayatri Mantra*' due to its metre.

3. '*Medha Jnana*': For three days after the '*Upanayana*' ritual, the student was said to remain in an embryonic condition. It was on the fourth day that his spiritual birth took place. The preceptor, who was now in the position of a father, then performed the '*Medha Jnana*' ceremony for sharpening the intellect, memory and grasping power of the student. Prayers were offered that the student should be favoured with an intelligence as attractive as cows and as brilliant as solar rays.
4. '*Utsarjan*' *Ceremony*: This ceremony marked the culmination of an academic session. It was performed in the month of '*Magh*', i.e., January-February.
5. '*Vedaramba*' *Ceremony*: This ceremony was marked at the commencement of the studies of the Vedas, Vedangas etc. The age at which this, ceremony was performed varied between fifteen years to twenty years.

6. *'Kasanta or Golden Ceremony'*: The student was reminded once again of his vow of *'Brahmacharya'* (Celibacy).
7. *'Samvartana' Ceremony*: It marked the termination of student life. It implied 'returning home' from the Guru's house. It was in a way passport to join the *'Grahastha Ashram'* (Family Life).

COMPARISON BETWEEN THE EDUCATIONAL OBJECTIVES IN VEDIC INDIA AND MODERN INDIA

1. *All Round Development:* Main Aim of Education. The main aim of education was all round development in India and the same aim is kept in view in modern education. The ancient educator never neglected physical development although he insisted on spiritual and intellectual development also at the same time. He always ensured a very clean, attractive and natural environment, far away from the towns and villages, to his students. Although we profess to look after physical, moral, spiritual, emotional and intellectual development of the student in a modern school yet it is the bookish knowledge which gets the most of our attention. But in ancient schools this ideal of all-round development was adhered to.
2. *Education for Democracy*: The educator was democratic in his approach in the field of education. All the students, rich or poor, princes or commoners, were treated alike. Lord Krishna and Sudama were at par in the ancient school in India. Of course, at present democracy has several dimensions.
3. *Education for Self-Suficiency:* Modern education lays much stress on self-sufficiency. The ancient school followed this principle by and large. The school was a small integrated community, self-sufficient in every way. The students themselves grew food products, tended cows, collected fire woods and elected the cottages for the

whole school community under the guidance of their teacher.

4. *Education for All.* Education was universal. It was free also. The fees if any were due to be paid after attaining education from the earnings of the young man who got education. It was in the form of *'Guru Dakshina'*. During education, board and lodging was free for almost all students. Socially every person was required to provide education to his young ones.

Points of Contrast

1. *Community Life*: The school in ancient India was a residential institution. All the students had to reside in their educational institutions for a long time. The school was a small community. But there is no such thing in a modern school. The pupils stay in the school for about six hours a day on working days only.
2. *Contact of Pupils and Teachers*: In ancient India there was full family life in the hermitage of the teacher. The teacher was revered as a father and his wife the mother for all the pupils. As it was always a residential school, there were better opportunities of intimate teacher-pupil relations. The teacher taught not one or two subjects. He was the only teacher of the child and that too for a long period. He was not a coach or a trainer but an educator. Contrary to this, the teacher of the modern school seldom knows the names of all his students. He is responsible for achievement of results and that too in his own subject. If a student is successful in his subject but fails in all the other subjects, it is not of much concern to him.
3. *More Emphasis on Education for Other Worldliness*: In ancient schools, although the teacher looked after the all-round development of the students yet he laid more stress for happiness in the other world. The highest

wisdom was to seek release from worldly desires.

4. *Methods of Teaching*: Cramming was very popular in ancient schools though other methods were also used. But now-a-days we lay more stress on inductive and heuristic methods.
5. *Discipline*: There was adequate provision for recreation on account of the nearness of natural environment in ancient schools. But the notion of play way in education did not exist. The whole educational programme was pursued seriously. Discipline was very hard.
6. *Examination*: The teacher himself was the examiner unlike the present system of education.
7. *Value Education*: In ancient education, value education received an important attention.

Other Aspects of Vedic Education and Modern Education

In going through the various aspects of education one cannot but be struck by the similarity of most of the problems dealt with by '*sutrakars*' in those times and the problems still facing educationists all over the world today, such as the period of instruction, the teacher pupil ratio, the pupil teacher relationship, the emoluments of the teachers, discipline, examination system, etc. We find that on almost all these, the ancients had arrived at solutions which even the moderners find it difficult.

The ancient system of dividing society into four groups of '*varnas*' based on their aptitude and occupations led to 25% of the students of the relevant age group pursuing for higher studies. We now find that the proportion of students going for higher studies, namely, university education even in the advanced countries is not more than 25%. In regard to the vexed question of teacher's emolument it appears that the ancients had arrived at the truth of the matter when they concluded that society would probably never be able to pay the teachers adequately in terms of money, and, therefore, all that the person adopting the teacher's life should expect, was austere life with ample respect from his pupils.

Evaluation was completely internal and depended upon the teacher. It was continuous evaluation and not yearly. The modern education also advocates internal evaluation.

It is generally accepted even now that residential schools have an important place in the system of education.

Of late, there has been a grave realisation that value education should be given an important place in the system of education. As compared with the Vedic system of education, modern education lays more emphasis on vocational education.

Modern terminology like education for democracy, education for socialism, education for secularism, education for emotional and national integration and education for international understanding etc. was non-existent in the Vedic system of education. Perhaps this was not needed at that time.

3

The Buddhist Education

INTRODUCTION

Buddhism came into being when several ills had crept into Vedic/Brahmanical Thought or Hinduism.

Mahatma Buddha's was a great charismatic personality. Perhaps in the world, there are only two instances of Mahatma Buddha and Swami

Mahavira—the two princes who renounced their princely and worldly life and devoted themselves to preach Buddhism and Jainism respectively.

Mahatma Buddha's philosophy of Buddhism is very simple. He laid great emphasis on leading a pure life. He avoided reference to metaphysics which he considered to be superfluous.

Buddhism is either silent or does not give importance to philosophical thinking on matters like God and Transmigration of Soul, etc.

Buddhism does not accept the 'Divinity' of the Vedas.

Mahatma Buddha practised several types of penances for finding out the truth.

SOURCES OF INFORMATION ABOUT BUDDHIST EDUCATION

The following Buddhist literature provides information on Buddhist education:

1. *'Pitakas'*: For a long time, the teachings of Buddha were transmitted through the regular succession of scholars and their disciples. They were reduced to writing only in about 80 B.C. during the reign of King Vattaghamani in Ceylon (Sri Lanka). The three *'Pitakas'* (meaning the baskets containing written palm leaves on the philosophy of Buddhism) were given their final shape. The Pitakas are in Pali language—the language of the common man.

   The *'Pitakas'* have the following three divisions:

   (i) *'Sutta'* or Tales.

   (ii) *'Vinnay'* or Discipline.

   (iii) *'Abhidamma'* or Doctrine.
2. The *'Milinda Panha'* (Question of King Malinda): It is a dialogue between the Buddhist scholar and teacher Nagarsena and the great King Mendander (125-95 B.C.) who ruled in some parts of India—North-Western Frontier Province, Sindh and Punjab.
3. The *'Jatakas'*: The Jatakas are a collection of 551 legends, riddles and stories on the life of Buddha. In each story, Buddha appears in one of his previous carnation—various births in various forms—priest, prince, *'deva'*, slave, woman, animal and bird etc.

PHILOSOPHY OF BUDDHISM AND TEACHING OF BUDDHA

The teachings of Buddha is the Buddhist philosophy. Its main tenets are:

1. Four Noble Truths.
2. Eight-fold Path for Attainment of *'Nirvana'* (Salvation).
3. Moral Code: Importance of Good Deeds in Life.
4. Middle Path: Avoidance of Extreme Form of Austerity and Luxury.

5. Equality – No Caste System.
6. *'Ahimsa'* (Non-violence).
7. Silence over the Existence of God.
8. No belief in rituals.
9. Belief in Rebirth and *'Karma'*.

Four-Noble Truths

Buddha renounced the pleasures of princely life and practised severe penances for finding out the truth of life. He saw the following four noble truths:

(i) All existence involves suffering.
(ii) Suffering is caused by desire, especially the desire for the continuance of existence.
(iii) The suppression of desire leads to the extinction of suffering.
(iv) The deliverance can be effected by the eight-fold path which consists of:

Eight-Fold Path

1. *Right View or Belief* – It includes the knowledge of misery, the origin of misery, the cessation of misery and the path leading to the cessation of misery.
2. *The Right Resolve* – To renounce sexual pleasure, to have malice towards none, to be harsh to no one.
3. *Right Speech* – To abstain from falsehood, backbiting, harsh language and frivolous talk.
4. *Right Behaviour* – To abstain from taking that which is not given and from immorality.
5. *Right Occupation* – Livelihood which does not involve ostensible evil.
6. *Right Effort* – To abandon existing evil qualities and to follow good qualities.
7. *Right Contemplation* – Clear observation.
8. *Right Concentration* – Control of senses and mind.

BASIC PRINCIPLES OF THE PHILOSOPHY OF EDUCATION AS BASED ON THE PHILOSOPHY OF BUDDHISM

1. *Primacy of Mind in all Man's Thought and Action*: Throughout his life Mahatma Buddha demonstrated by his conduct and the clarity of his thought that path to self-realisation, i.e., Nirvana—the objective of life, lay through the purity of mind. The magnificent opening verses of the '*Dhamapada*' state.

मनोपुब्बङ्गमा धम्मा मनोसेट्ठा मनोमया।

मनसा चे पदुट्ठेन भासति वा करोति वा।

ततो नं दुःखमन्वेति चक्कंव वहतो पदम्।।

Mind is the forerunner of all mental phenomena. They have mind as their chief, they are mind-made. If one speaks or acts with an evil mind, *dukkha* follows him just as the wheel follows the hoof-print of the ox that draws the cart.

The second verse states:

मनोपुब्वंगमा धम्मा मनोसेट्ठा मनोमया।

मनसा चे पसन्नेन भासति वा करोति वा।

ततो पं सुखमन्वेति छायाव अनपायिनी।।

Mind is the forerunner of all mental phenomena. They have mind as their chief, they are mind-made. If one speaks or acts with a pure mind, happiness ('*Sukha*') follows him like a shadow that never leaves him.

2. *Application of Reason and Logic*: Buddha exhorted the people to apply the standards of reason and logic to all philosophies, ideas, and practice, including his own. In the *Anguttara Nikaya*, Buddha said to the Kalama people:

एस तुम्हे, कालमा, मा अनुस्सवेन, मा परम्पराय, मा इतिकिरियाय,

मा पिटकसम्पदानेन, मा तक्कहेतु, मा भयहेतु, मा आकारपरिवितक्केन

मा भब्बरूपताय, मा समणो नो गरूति।

यदा तुम्हे, कालामा, अत्तनाव जानेय्याथ–'इमे धम्मा अकुसला, इमे धम्मा सावज्जा।

Do not accept any teaching merely because you have heard it from someone, or because it is sanctioned by tradition, or because you believe it to be your duty, or because it is stated in the scriptures, or by force of arguments, or because someone tells you that this is the path, or because of form or the beauty of form, or because you feel that the '*Sramana*' is your '*guru*'. When you yourselves from your own experience find that certain conduct is sinful and produces suffering and harm, then discard this conduct.

Such was Buddha's belief in the supremacy of rational thought that he asked the people not to accept even his own teachings unquestioningly. In the Sanyukta Nikaya he said:

तापाच्छेदाच् च निकषात् सुवर्णमिव पण्डितैः।

परीक्ष्य भिक्षवो ग्राह्यं मद्वचो न तु गौरवात्।।

Just as experts melt, beat and test gold for its purity so also O '*bhikkus*', examine my own teachings in diverse ways. Accepts them only if you find them to be valid. Do not accept them without examining them simply because they are my teachings.

MAIN FEATURES OF BUDDHIST EDUCATION

Buddhism believed that the world was full of sorrow and that salvation could be obtained only by renouncing it. In the beginning it took to the education of monks only. When later on it took up the education of the masses it did not present any important points of difference from those of Hinduism. Both systems had similar ideals and followed similar methods. The difference was only visible in religious and social ideology, the types of schools and in the provision made for girls' education.

I. *Aims of Education*. Following were the main aims of education:

1. Development of moral character.
2. Religious and spiritual development.
3. Promotion of social efficiency.
4. Promotion of Culture.

II. *Ceremonies Associated with Education*. Among the important ceremonies, following deserve special mention.

1. *Phahajja Ceremony* or *Ordination or Initiation Ceremony*. The injunction of Buddha that every novice should be trained in the discipline and doctrine of religion resulted in making Buddhist monasteries centres of learning. An entrant, if he was less than eight, had to perform the '*Phahajja*' (going forth) ceremony. It was similar to the '*Upanayana*' ceremony. For entry, the permission of parents was essential. The novice got his hair cut and then went to the monastery of his choice. He had a robe of yellow clothes with him and approached the elder of monastery for initiation. The novice had to take an oath, "I take refuge with the Buddha, I take refuge with the Religion. I take refuge with the Order." He was also administered ten commandments, viz.,

(i) Not taking life.
(ii) Taking what is given.
(iii) Abstaining from impure practices.
(iv) Not telling a lie.
(v) Not drinking.
(vi) Not eating out of time.
(vii) Not dancing, singing and seeing shows.
(viii) Not using garlands, scents, ornaments, etc.
(ix) Not using high or large couch.
(x) Not receiving gold and silver.

The novitiate period was of twelve years duration. The life of a novice was like that of a '*Brahmachari*' of Brahmanical order. He had to beg his daily food and had to do all manual and menial work connected with monastic life of cleaning clothes and utensils, bringing water, supervision of stores etc. The rules and discipline of the Order had to be obeyed strictly. In case of a serious breach of discipline, the student was expelled from the Order.

2. '*Upasampada*' *Ceremony*. The second ceremony called the '*Upasampada*' was performed after the end of the novitiate period and the student at that time had to be not less than twenty years old. After this ceremony he became a full-fledged monk or '*Bhikshu*'.

He was taught to:

(i) beg his food;
(ii) wear robes made of rags;
(iii) lodge at the foot of a tree;
(iv) use cows urine as a medicine;
(v) avoid sex, theft and taking life.

If he violated any of these rules he was expelled from the order. The period of '*Upasampada*' was ten years and then he became an Acharya who could himself receive pupils.

III. *Primary Education*: There is sufficient evidence to show that popular education was widespread when Buddhist monasteries flourished. Even those who did not intend joining the Buddhist Sangha, attended the school up to the age of twelve and received instruction in 4 R's (reading, writing, arithmetic and religion). It is evident that Buddhist monastery played an important part in supplying popular elementary education.

Hieun Tsang and Itsing visited India in the 7th century A.D. They have given a good account of popular primary education.

They say that education commenced at the age of six. After finishing the first book Siddhirastu, the child was introduced to Vyakarana (Grammar), Hetu Vidya (Logic), Nyaya (Science of Reasoning), Adhyatima Vidya (Inner Science), Silpasthan Vidya (Arts and Crafts) and Chikitsa Vidya (Medicine).

IV. *The Curriculum*: The curriculum was primarily religious and philosophical as it was chiefly meant for monks and nuns. They were not taught secular sciences like poetics, literature and astrology. After his admission the novice was taught Pali and Sanskrit for ten years and then the study of Tripataken was undertaken. After this, works on Buddhist religion and philosophy were mastered. They also studied Hindu system of religion, logic and philosophy in order to carry on disputations and discussions with Hindu theologians.

While included in the curriculum, the Vedas were not the basis of Buddhist education. Buddhist literature replaced them as the source of wisdom and morality. Sanskrit was their chief language, though not the medium of instruction.

Subjects Relating to Buddhism

1. Buddhist literature.
2. Functional knowledge of the Constitution of the monasteries *'Vihars'*.

Subjects of Brahmanical Education

(i) The Vedas
(ii) The Puranas
(ii) Grammar
(iv) Rhetorics
(v) Systems of Philosophy
(vi) Yoga
(vii) Military Science
(viii) Hymns

Other Subjects

1. Magical and mystical formulas.
2. Medicine.
3. Sexual science.
4. Knowledge of the sounds of animals.

(For details see University of Nalanda).

5. *Educational Institutions.* Buddhist education was centred round a monastery. There were some private teachers who took ten to fifteen children and taught them in their houses. The rise of the organised educational institutions may be attributed to the influence of Buddhism.

6. *Education of Women.* Lord Buddha allowed the women to join his Sangha. This resulted in the emancipation of women. Women of aristocratic and commercial communities began to pursue eternal truths of religion and philosophy. Some of them led a life of celibacy and went outside India to preach Buddhism. Up to the 4th century A.D., extensive educational opportunities were provided for girls.

7. *Methods of Instruction.*

(i) *Oral Instruction.* The teacher gave lessons to the students who learnt them by heart. Thereafter he put questions to them.

(ii) *Discussion.* For the promotion of Buddhism, it was essential to impress the general public. Therefore, the power of discussion was developed. Rules for discussion were framed and followed strictly.

Itsing gives a detailed account of the manner in which teaching-learning was conducted in India. The teacher gave lessons to his students in such a way that he did not pass over any fact without giving its full explanation. The teaching-learning process was far from being mere cramming of texts. Reasoning and analysis formed an important part. Itsing admires the remarkable powers of explanation and exposition of the Indian teachers. He observed, "A place was also given to discussions and debates, at least in the higher part of the course and pupil's ability seems to have been very largely assessed by his power to defeat his opponents in debates and discussions. It was such individuals who got royal appointments and whose names were as a reward, inscribed in lofty gates."

(iii) *Evidences*. For finding out the truth, evidences of eight kinds was required.

(a) *'Siddhanta'* (theory)

(b) *'Hetu'* (Reason)

(c) *'Udaharan'* (Exemplification or citation)

(d) *'Sadharma'* (Parallalism)

(e) *'Vaidharmya'* (Contradiction)

(f) *'Pratyakash'* (Cognisable and tangible)

(g) *'Anumaan'* (Inference or analogy)

(h) *'Agamavva'* (Induction)

4. *Vidwat Sabha* (Learned Conference)

5. *Ekant Sadhna* (Solitary Meditation)

6. *Tours*

8. *Buddhistic Monasteries*: They may be called the counterparts of Gurukuls of the Brahmanic system. A Buddhistic monastery of a Vihara was a federation of individual schools, each under an Acharya. These individual schools had developed a sort of collective life and a code of discipline and regulations which was binding upon all the units. All these units maintained harmonious relations, helping each other in times of need. No Acharya could draw the pupils of another Acharya.

The monasteries were maintained by the endowments of the laity, kings and merchants. These persons built the Viharas and attached to them fields, houses, gardens and orchards.

Sometimes the daily food was also supplied by the laity. According to Hieun Tsang there were 5000 monasteries in the 7th century A.D.

9. *Buddhist Universities*: Some Buddhist monasteries developed into great centres of learning and came to be known as universities. Brahmanic system of education was not so rich in having many universities as the Buddhist system had. There were seven well-known universities, viz., Nalanda, Vallabhai, Vikramsila, Jagaddala, Mithila, Odantapuri and Nadia. Of all these Nalanda was the greatest and most famous.

A Buddhist University was under the charge of an eminent Bhikshu, reputed for his character, age and scholarship. The chief Bhikshu was helped by two councils—academic and administrative. The first council was responsible for making admissions, determining courses, assigning work to different teachers and arranging for examinations at the end of the courses. Construction and repair of buildings, distribution of food, clothes and medicine, allotment of rooms in the hostel and assignment of monastic work fell within the jurisdiction of the administrative council. The council had also to provide finances through various methods and means.

These universities had huge buildings of their own for lecture halls and for residence purposes. For example, at Nalanda, there were eight big lecture halls, 300 class-rooms, three big libraries and a large number of residential rooms.

10. *Lodging and Boarding Arrangements*: The *Jatakas* inform us that several hostels existed at various universities. In these hostels there were common messes run by the authorities. Excavation carried out at Nalanda reveals that students were provided with stone benches to sleep upon and niches for keeping lamps and other sundry things. Some universities used to provide free clothing and medicines. Sometimes, hospitals/ dispensaries were also maintained for the hosteler.

11. *Mass Education: The Education of Community*. At first

Buddhist education was purely monastic and was intended only for those who entered the order. In course of time it was realised that it was necessary to win public sympathy and support for the spread of the gospal and the best way to spread the gospal was to undertake the education of the young when the mind is pliable. There was thus a better chance of both recruiting proper types of persons for the order and of getting so many sympathisers and supporters. So the educational effort was extended to the whole community. "Buddhism, therefore, threw itself heart and soul into the cause of general education of the whole community from about the beginning of the Christian era".

12. *Corporate Institutions:* The most noteworthy development of the Buddhist education was the rise of corporate institutions of higher studies. Such institutions were first developed probably in the 5th century A.D. The Buddhist monasteries developed into big establishments and began to cater to the education of the laity as well, besides the Buddhist monks and the novices. About 10 percent of the Buddhist monasteries provided higher education. Taking a leaf out of Buddhist monasteries, temple colleges came into existence at about the 8th century A.D. These temple colleges imparted higher Sanskrit studies.

The corporate educational institutions had a tremendous influence on educational practices. Governing bodies came into being and decided courses in the institutions. Now a student became a member of an educational community where scores of teachers and hundreds of students lived and learned together. Students studied several subjects from different teachers, each specialised in his own field. Usually free boarding and lodging were provided at these corporate institutions. The environment here facilitated learning and produced great authors and scholars of world-wide fame.

13. *Monitorial System*: About the students of the University

of Valabhi (in Kathiawar), the Chinese pilgrim Itsing observes that they used to spend two or three years "instructed by their teachers and instructing others". Senior students at Taxila were often put incharge of the students during the temporary absence of their teachers.

14. *Admission Procedure to Higher Education*: In ancient Indian education system, every student who sought admission to a higher course, had to undergo a stiff test to prove that he was fit for it. Morally disqualified students were summarily rejected. (*Nirukla* II. 4). In famous universities like Nalanda, out of ten only two or three aspirants of higher education could succeed in getting admission.

In *Indian Teachers of Buddhist Universities*: Bose mentions that at Nalanda and Vikramsila there were '*durapalas*' (door keepers) or learned professors appointed to regulate admission by testing the calibre, capacity and sincerity of the applicants for admission. Probably similar arrangements were also in vogue in other institutions of higher learning.

From the stories as mentioned in various Jatakas, the admission at Taxila was open to all with no entrance test. On the basis of Jatakas 272, 285, 324 and 436, S. Narain (1993) explains the rationale of no test in these words, "It appears that one of the considerations for the open door policy had been that the aspirant student had to travel a distance of hundreds and even thousands of miles to reach Taxila. With no means of transport available in those days it would take months to complete the journey which was sometime perlious also. It is only the intensive desire and sincerity to peruse advanced study and the willingness to make sacrifice in terms of comfort, luxury, etc. which brought the students at the portal of the college at Taxila. Such being the case, denial of admission would have been grossly unfair to a true seeker of knowledge".

15. *Buildings of Educational Institutions*: We have definite evidence to show that the Buddhist universities and temple

colleges of the Hindus had spacious buildings for the classrooms and hostels. There were big lecture halls at Nalanda and Vikramsila Universities.

As far as private teachers were concerned they usually held their classes in their own houses.

16. *Private Enterprise*: Private enterprise had all along been the sheet anchor of the ancient Indian educational system. Of course, there were no organisations running educational institutions, private enterprise was synonymous with individual private teachers. As a matter of fact each learned teacher was an educational institution by himself. Corporate educational institutions came into being in ancient India with the establishment of Buddhist monasteries. When Buddhist monasteries developed into big establishments from the time of Asoka onwards, they naturally developed into centres of 'learning' and education. Hindu educational institutions, so far known, are all later than the time of Nalanda University. Temple colleges started by the Hindus were a natural reaction to the Buddhist monastic universities.

The '*charans*'—sort of literary organisations, formed by the followers of the Vedas in ancient India, prior to the Buddhist period were merely a loose organisation based on the fellowship of students and teachers working at different centres.

17. *Teacher-Pupil Relations During the Buddhist Period:* An excerpt from Itsing reads as, "He (the teacher) supervises pupil's moral conduct and warns him of defects and transgressions; whenever he finds his pupils faulty, he makes him seek remedies and repent."

Following were the important duties of a teacher:

First, the teacher must give the pupil under his charge all possible intellectual and spiritual guidance by teaching, by putting questions to him, by exhortation and by instruction.

Second, where the pupil did not have necessary articles such as an alms-bowl or a robe, the teacher would supply that out of his own belongings.

Third, if the pupil falls ill, the teacher must nurse him.

The Buddhist system of education, like the Brahmanical system enjoins upon the pupil the duty of serving his teacher as a part of education. Following duties were prescribe for the pupil.

1. To rise early from bed and to give his teacher teeth cleaner and water to rinse his month.
2. To prepare a seat for the teacher, serving him rice-milk in rinsed jug and after his drinking it, wash the vessel and sweep the place.
3. To equip the teacher for his begging round by giving him fresh undergarment, girdle, his two upper garments and his alms-bowl rinsed and filled with water.
4. Equipping the pupil himself like the teacher if he wants to accompany him.
5. Not to interrupt his teacher while he speaks, even if he makes a mistake.
6. To sweep the Vihara where his teacher dwells.
7. Not to give or receive anything without his teacher's permission.
8. Not to enter the village without his teacher's permission.
9. To nurse the teacher when he is sick.

The monks or the Buddhist ascetics who imparted education during the period of the Buddhist ascendancy, were a select band of teachers who had undergone a severe training themselves and they could come from any class. "As the great streams, O disciples, however many they may be, the Ganga, Yamuna, Saraju, Mahi, when they reach the great ocean, lose their old name and their old descent, and bear only one name, 'the great ocean', so also my disciples, these four castes, nobles, Brahmans, Vaishyas and Sudras, when they, in accordance with the law and doctrine which the perfect one has preached, forsake their home and go into homelessness, lost their old name and old paternity, and bear only the one destination, 'Ascetics', who follow the son of the Sakya house. (*Chulluvagga*, IX, 1.4).

According to *Mahavagga* (I. 28, 84), a teacher was expected to be fully versed in what belongs to moral practices, self-concentration, wisdom, emancipation and the knowledge and insight thereto; must be able to help others with full perfection in these; must be modest, fearful of sinning, strenuous, of ready memory, not guilty of transgressions in moral conduct; and must be able to train a pupil in the precepts of proper conduct, to educate him in the elements of morality, to instruct him in what pertains to the 'Vinaya', to discuss or to make another discuss according to Dhamma a false doctrine that might arise."

Apart from teaching, a Buddhist monk had to give discourses to the people who gathered to learn from him the principles of Dhamma.

18. *High Code of the Teaching Profession*: According to *Millanda-panha*, the teacher was required to teach everything he knew to his disciple; he could withhold nothing under the apprehension that the disciple may one day outshine him in his profession. How generous and large-hearted teachers usually were in this connection can be judged from the conduct and exclamation of Alara Kalama, when the father Bhikshu had finished his education under him: "Happy friend are we in that we look upon such a venerable one, such a fellow ascetic as you. The doctrine which I know, you too know, and the doctrine which you know, I too know. As I am, so you are. As you are, so am I. Pray, let us be joint wardens of this company." (quoted by Altekar)

EDUCATIONAL IMPLICATIONS OF BUDDHIST PHILOSOPHY

The entire teachings of Buddhism provide directions to develop good conduct which is also the essence of a sound system of education. To be a moral being, one must follow the noble path. Eight-fold path as preached by Buddha provides guidance for moral education and peace. Observance of purity is more important than the observance of rituals.

The curriculum was primarily religious and philosophical. The Vedas were not the basis of Buddhist education. Buddhist literature replaced them as the source of wisdom and morality. The teacher and the student were united together by mutual affection and confidence. Buddha did not want that his teachings and the teachings of others should be followed blindly. He greatly emphasised that all aspects of a phenomena should be reflected upon and pros and cons taken into account. He was in fact a fore-runner of scientific tendencies in education. Reason should be the basis of our belief.

Buddhism promoted mother-tongue as the medium of education.

Buddhism contributed a lot to the spread of education. Hieun Tsang, the great Chinese philosopher and scholar who visited India in the 7th century A.D. has paid high tributes to Indian system of education and learning. A large number of Universities or Institutes of Learning sprang up where students from foreign lands came in large numbers to quench their thirst for knowledge. There were seven well-established universities: Nalanda, vallabhai, Vikramsila, Jagdala, Mithila, Odantapuri and Nadia. Of all these Nalanda was the greatest and the most famous.

Summing Up

In the words of Altekar, "Buddhism may well be proud of its contribution to the cause of education in ancient India. Its colleges threw their doors open to all, irrespective of any considerations of caste or country. The rise of organised public educational institutions may be justly attributed to its influence. It raised the international status of India by the efficiency of its higher education, which attracted students from distant countries like Korea, China, Tibet and Java. The cultural sympathy which the countries in eastern Asia feel for India even today is entirely due to the work of the famous Buddhist colleges of ancient India. If some of the important lost texts can be recovered from Tibet or China or can be reconstructed with the help of Tibetan or Chinese translations, the credit must be given to Buddhist colleges, which enabled Chinese students to get their copies. Buddhist education also helped the development of Hindu logic and philosophy by initiating and encouraging comparative study. In the period of its early history, it championed the cause of education through the mother tongue; later on however it could not resist the charm and influence of Sanskrit and began to impart education through that language.

4

Religion-Oriented Ancient Education

Institutes of Higher Learning in Vedic and Buddhist Period

RELIGIOUS ENVIRONMENT AND EDUCATION IN ANCIENT INDIA

1. Every aspect of life including education in ancient India was influenced by religion in ancient India. However, it must be remembered that education aimed at the many sided development of the personality of the student of course with a religious orientation. The concept, aims and ideals of education were correlated with the ideals of life. Religion played an important role in life in ancient India. The whole of social structure of those days was religious. It was to a great extent independent of government. "Governments may come and go but social life, religious life and national culture were not much affected by these changes." Not only political but even the economic changes could not affect the religious aspect of education.

The whole of educational system surged with religious atmosphere. Teachers were usually priests. It is, therefore, no wonder that the infusion of a spirit of religiousness in the minds of the pupils should have been regarded as the first and foremost aim of education.

Following were the important religious ceremonies ('*Sanskars*') associated with the system of education of each student.

1. *'Vidyaramba Sanskar'*
2. *'Upanayan Sanskar'*
3. *'Medha Sanskar'*
4. *'Utsarjan Sanskar'*
5. *'Vedaramba Sanskar'*
6. *'Kasanta Sanskar'*
7. *'Samvartna Sanskar'*

(These *'Sanskars'* are explained in Chapter 2)

2. *Life of Purity*: Spiritual Development. A student had to observe religious observance during his educational course. Students were to observe strict celibacy in speech and thought. It was believed that strength of mind and character developed if we learn to deny to ourselves our natural desires and inclinations; foods like meat, sweetmeats, spices and ornaments were prohibited. Even staying royal students were not allowed to have any private purse lest they should secretly purchase prohibited articles. Plain living and high thinking was to be the student's ideal.

3. *Prayer*: Students had to offer daily morning and evening prayers. Vedic students used to spend a good deal of the morning time in performing various morning rituals connected with the fire sacrifices; they gave them practical training in the rituals they were expected to perform in their after life. At sunset they offered usual prayers and attended to fire sacrifices.

4. *Begging of Food*: The begging of the daily food has been enjoined in the student life as a religious duty. We find this injunction in sacred texts from the Vedic age downwards. The Buddhist monks also moved from place to place for alms.

5. *Celebration of Religious Festivals*: Religious festivals were celebrated in the monastery or the preceptor's house almost every month.

All these rituals and observances fostered piety in the mind of the young student. Thus a spiritual background was provided which could enable a student to withstand the temptations of life. Spiritual development by penance was their cherished ideal. In orders to gain spiritual merit, good conduct was greatly emphasised. Yajnavalkya Smriti gives a comprehensive view of the components of conduct and character. 'Harmlessness, non-stealing, purity, control of the organs, self-control, mercy, forgiveness are the means of religion for all'. These virtues were inculcated

(i) By direct injunction of the teacher.
(ii) By living a life of industry, self-control, perseverance, penance, self-abnegation, temperance and continuance.

Spiritual development by means of 'Tapas' was their cherished ideal. The spiritual values of truth, beauty and goodness were pursued for their own sake by students in the Brahmanic period. In addition to daily prayers students had to do a lot of "Manan" (contemplation) and live a life of penances, austerities and hardships. Such practices not only fostered religious outlook in them but also helped them to realise spiritual values of life. The educational institutions had a religious and spiritual environment on account of the nobler character of the teacher. It was in such an environment that the young mind was nurtured.

During the Buddhist period, an entrant to a monastery which was also a place of education, had to take several moral vows.

COMPARISON BETWEEN VEDIC/BRAHMANICAL SYSTEM OF EDUCATION AND BUDDHIST SYSTEM OF EDUCATION

1. *Gurukul System and Monasterial System of Education*: Brahmanical system was a Gurukul system. The teacher's home was the school. The influence of home was considered as an indispensable educational factor. Under the Buddhist system the Guru's home was

replaced by the monastery. Buddhism wanted to give up domestic ties.

2. *Relationship Between the Teacher and the Taught*: Under the Brahmanical system the relationship between the teacher and the pupil and the control of the teacher over the pupil was deep. This was not so under the Buddhist system. In the monastery there was no distinction between the full-fledged monks except that of length of spiritual standing.
3. *Curriculum*: Curriculum is the Buddhistic system was not so comprehensive as compared to Brahmanic system and it was on the pattern of Brahmanic school. The Vedas were replaced by Buddhist scriptures.
4. *Religious and Moral-Education*: The Buddhists like the Brahmans placed their moral and religious ideal at the top. The basis of both types of education was religious, moral and intellectual discipline. As a matter of fact Buddhist educational ideals and practices were derived from those of the Brahmanic system.
5. *Coverage of Population*: Contribution of Buddhism to education was distinct. Buddhism enlarged educational opportunities for non-Brahman castes. There was a high degree of literacy. Tuition, board and lodging were free in all these schools though the students had to beg in order to support themselves and the monks.
6. *Status of Educational Institutions*: Buddhist centres of education attracted students from far and near and this raised the international status of India. They encouraged comparative study of logic and philosophy. With the advent of Buddhist system of education, the monopoly of Brahmanic Schools was broken. Buddhism threw open its institutions to all castes. Popular education, therefore, flourished.
7. *Contribution to Art, Architecture and Sculpture*: Promotion of Buddhism was marked by the development of art,

architecture and sculpture as fine images of Buddha and Budhisatvas began to be built.

8. *Foreign Contacts*: Spread of Buddhism encouraged foreign contacts. Several scholars from China and other countries came to India for visiting places associated with Mahatma Buddha. They also studied at Universities like Nalanda. In turn several Indian scholars went to other countries to promote Buddhist culture and thought. Brahmanical culture and learning also spread in foreign lands

CENTRES OF HIGHER LEARNING/UNIVERSITIES IN THE VEDIC AND BUDDHIST PERIOD

Introduction

Indian Institutes of Higher Learning as International Institutions of Higher Learning/Universities: Centuries before universities in Europe and other parts of the world came into existence, there flourished universities in India which had international reputation and attracted foreign students. The Products of these institutions were highly respected in their own countries. To use the present terminology, they took pride in calling themselves as 'India Returned'.

Chief Characteristics of Higher Education Institutions

Education in India was for a long time imparted by private teachers in their own houses. They were scattered all over the country but they congregated in large numbers in certain places on account of the facilities they got in their work. Such places were usually the capitals of kingdom or holy places. Kings and princes in those days were patrons of learning and so learned Brahmans were attracted to their courts. That is why Taxila, Kanauj, Patliputra, Mithila etc., became famous centres of learning. As the pilgrims supplied a subsidiary source of income to the famous teachers residing at holy places, these places became centres of learning, e.g., Banaras, Ranchi and Nasik, etc.

Buddhist monasteries existed as corporate bodies. As Buddhist education was at first confined to the education of monks, Buddhist monasteries developed into corporate educational institutions. Later on it was realised that the best way to propagate religion was to educate the rising generation which had pliable mind. The Buddhist monasteries, therefore, after taking up the education of the lay population became great centres of learning and came to be known as universities. They were Nalanda, Vallabhi, Vikramsila, Jagaddala, Odantapuri, Mithila and Nadia. Of all these Nalanda was the most famous and the greatest.

Organisation of Buddhist Universities: A Buddhist university was under the charge of an eminent Bhikshu, reputed for his character, age and scholarship. The office was elective. The chief Bhikshu or the principal officer was helped by two Councils; academic and administrative. The first Council was responsible for making admissions, determining courses, assigning work to different teachers and arranging for examinations at the end of courses. Construction and repair of buildings, distribution of food, clothes and medicine, allotment of rooms in the hostel and assignment of monastic work fell within the jurisdiction of the administrative council. This council had also to provide finances by various methods and means. These Universities had huge buildings of their own for lecture halls and for residential purposes.

Temple Colleges: As the Buddhist monasteries developed into great centres of learning, the Hindus also started Temple Colleges as a reaction to the Buddhist Universities. The 'Mathas' and the Acharyas of the medieval times continued the same tradition. The Temple Colleges were administered by the temple sub-committee of the village council. This sub-committee administered the estates given as endowments and appointed teachers of the institution. The head of the institution was incharge of internal administration.

Court Assemblies: Debating and learned disputations were the characteristic features of Indian intellectual life. These were usually held in courts under the patronage of the king. In these discussions, superior knowledge was "tested, rewarded, recognised and proclaimed". The kings rewarded talent with the grants of land. Such court assemblies were very frequent under the Brahmanic system of education and very common under the Buddhist kings who convened learned assemblies very frequently.

IMPORTANT CENTRES OF LEARNING (TEMPLE COLLEGES) IN SOUTH INDIA

Kanchi

Kanchi, the capital of the Pallava rules (4th to 7th century A.D.), became the Kashi (Banaras or Varanasi) of the South for its being famous seat of education, learning and cultural development. It also became the abode of great religious preachers and Sanskrit scholars. Hieun Tsang, the renowned Chinese pilgrim and scholar visited this place in 640 A.D. and observed, "the learner's were held in high esteem. Kanchi was a fine, well-built up city". There were one hundred and eight families who were totally engaged in the study of the Vedas and Vedic literature.

The Academy of Kanchi attracted scholars and students from different parts of the country. Several temples were built at Kanchi. Mukteswara was an important temple.

There was a celebrated college named Chatikasthana.

Koluru. There was an institute of higher learning at Koluru in Karnataka. There were two hundred students. It had a well-equipped '*Saraswati Bhandarika*' (Library).

Bahur

There was a flourishing college at Bahur near Pondicherry during the eighth century A.D. It was called '*Vidyasthana*'. Fourteen subjects were taught here. The Pallava rulers patronised it.

Saltogi (Bijapur District)

In the 8th century A.D., during the rule of the Rashtrakutas, there was a temple, the hall of which accommodated a Sanskrit College. In course of time as many as twenty-seven hostels came up for residence of its students who hailed from different areas. The institute received huge endowments. The villagers of the nearby village contributed funds at each marriage and *Upanayan* ceremony.

Ennayiran Temple College (South Arcott district)

Admission of Students and Curriculum: The admission of students was governed by the principle of the reservation of a fixed number of seats for different subjects. Thus, 75 seats were reserved for the Rigveda and the Yajurveda each, 40 seats for the Samaveda, 20 for the White Yajurveda, 10 for the Atharvaveda, Baudhayana Dharmasutra and Vedanta each, 25 for grammar, 35 for Mimansa and 40 for Rupavatara. The institution was thus predominantly a Vedic college.

Number of Teachers: For the Rigveda and the Yajurveda, there were three teachers each, for the Mimansa two, and for the rest of the subjects one each. There were 16 teachers for 340 students. The average number of students per teacher was about 21. Students therefore received individual attention and instructions. Big classes like those existing in modern colleges were unknown.

Maintenance Allowance to Students: The college supplied free boarding to students. Each Vedic student received about one seer of rice per day and this quantity was sufficient for the daily meals. He also received annually an allowance of about one eighth *tola* of gold, which was probably intended to cover the clothing expenses. The allowance for the students of grammar and philosophy was about 6 per cent higher; the reason for this preferential treatment is not clear.

The Salaries of Teachers: The normal allowance for the teachers of the college was about 16 seers of rice every day. The cost of an ordinary meal was about half a seer of rice; an ordinary Sanskrit teacher was thus getting as his salary about three times the amount necessary for the food expenses of a family of five. He was thus receiving a salary just sufficient for his normal family responsibilities. He was neither rolling in riches nor suffering from abject poverty.

Community Support: The local village community had endowed the college with 300 acres of landed property.

Tirumukkudal Temple College

General Organisation: During the 11th century, Venkatesh Perumal Temple at Tirumukkudal in Chingleput district was a very interesting institution, for it was running a college, a hostel and a hospital. The College was a smaller institution than the one at Ennayiram, for arrangement was here made for the free boarding and lodging of 60 students only. Out of the 60 seats in the hostel, 10 were reserved for the students of the Rigveda, 10 for those of the Yajurveda, 20 for those of grammar, 10 for those of the Pancha-ratra system, 3 for those of Saivagama and 7 for Vanaprasthas and Sanyasins. All the students in the hostel were provided with oil for bath every Saturday.

Teachers' Salaries: The teachers' salaries in this institution were lower than those in the Ennayiram.

Tiruvorriyur Temple College (Chengalpattu District)

The college started in the memory of the great grammarian Panini was located in a big hall adjoining the local Siva temple.

There was a tradition current in the locality, that God Siva had appeared in this very temple before Panini for fourteen continuous days in order to teach him the first fourteen aphorisms. The village community had therefore organised an efficient grammar college in the Siva temple to commemorate the event. The college was a much bigger institution than the Ennayiram College. In the latter place, an endowment of 300 acres had enabled the organisers to arrange for the free food and education of 340 students. The Tiruvorriyur college had received an endowment of 400 acres. This grammar college had more than 450 students on its rolls. The number of teachers was probably about 20 to 25. This college went on performing its functions down to the 14th century.

Malkapuram Temple College

A Temple, College, Hostel and Hospital combined. An inscription from Malkapuram, dated 1268 A.D. reveals the existence of an institution which was a temple, a college, a hostel and a hospital combined. There were eight teachers in the college, four of the Vedas and Agamas and four for secular subjects consisting of grammar, literature and logic. There was one doctor incharge of the hospital. About 20 students on the average were under the charge of each teacher. The Malkapuram college had probably about 150 students. They were as usual offered free tuition, boarding, lodging and medicine.

Teachers' Pay: Each teacher was given as endowment of two *puttis* of land. The teacher's income was twice the wages of the skilled artisan. The society was offering him just what was necessary for a decent family life. There were several Temple Colleges in India. We have mentioned only some prominent ones.

SEATS OF HIGHER LEARNING IN INDIA (OTHER THAN TEMPLE COLLEGES)

Kashi (Banaras)

As it took centuries for the Vedic religion to penetrate to United Provinces, Bihar and Bengal, Banaras did not figure as a centre of learning in the Vedic period. In the Upanishadic period Banaras became a centre of Aryan religion and culture. In the 7th century B.C. Banaras was probably the most famous centre of education in eastern India. Under Ashoka, the Sarnath monastery must have become a famous seat of learning. It had about 1500 monk students. There is ample evidence to show that Banaras continued to be a centre of Buddhist learning down to the 12th century A.D.

Its learned Brahmans continued to promote the cause of education in the traditional manner. Banaras and Kashmir were the most famous centres of learning in India in the 11th century A.D.

Some scholars from Maharashtra and Karnataka came to Banaras in the 6th century and their descendants continued to dominate Banaras' scholars for about three centuries. Some Muslim rulers like Akbar, Shah Jahan and Dara extended their patronage to Banaras scholars. In medieval times the course of learning went on flourishing and the credit goes to Banaras Brahmans. Bernier says, "Banaras is a kind of University but it has no college or regular classes as in our universities and resembles rather the school of the ancients, the masters being spread over the different parts of the town in private houses. Some teachers have four and some six disciples, the most eminent may have twelve or fifteen but this is the largest number."

Kashmir

Kashmir was an important centre of international learning when Buddhism was flourishing in Central Asia. The famous

Buddhist scholar Kumarajiva had travelled from Khotan to Kashmir in order to study there fore two years. A Chinese scholar, O'kong, came to Kashmir and studied at Muktipadavihara in Hushkapura (Stein, *Itinery of O'kong*, p. 5). Intellectual traffic however was not only one way; Kashmir Buddhists also went out abroad to spread the gospel of the Sakya sage. Most famous among them was Gunavarman, who flourished in the 5th century A.D. Though belonging to a princely family, he discarded temporal prospects and pleasures, entered the holy orders and first went to Ceylon and then to Java. There he received an invitation from the Chinese emperor and went to China and spent his life there.

Mithila (Videha)

It was a renowned seat of learning in ancient times. In the Upanishads it remained a stronghold of Brahmanical culture. At that time the name of Mithila was Videha under the famous philosopher King Janak. Under the Kameshwara dynasty (1330-1515 A.D.) Mithila became famous for its versatile scholar Jagaddhara and the great poet Vidyapati. Mithila made profound contribution in the field of logic by developing a school of Nyaya under the great logicians Gangesha, Vardhamana and Pakshadhara. Mithila instituted a peculiar system of examination for graduation, known as '*shalakapariksha*'. A needle was pierced through the pages of a manuscript, and last page pierced was taken up to test the candidate's mastery of the subject. It implied a thorough understanding of each line of the text studied.

Nadia

It came to prominence during the reign of Lakshmana Sena (1106-1138 A.D.). Scholars like Halayudha (the learned Prime Minister) and Shulapani (an authority on law) and poets like Jayadeva (author of Gita-Govinda), Dhoyi and Umapati built up the reputation of Nadia. After the destruction of Buddhist

Viharas at Nalanda and Vikramasila, Nadia got the opportunity of renewing Brahmanical learning. The need for a new centre of learning in Bengal was urgently felt as Mithila rigidly guarded its treasure of knowledge and did not permit any scholar to take away any manuscript or notes beyond its boundary. Vasudeva Sarvabhuma of Nadia first met the challenge by committing to memory two important books during his study at Mithila and reducing them to writing on his return to Nadia.

Nalanda

One of the Earliest Universities in the World. The Nalanda University, one of the most famous and world's earliest university flourished till 12th century A.D. It is described as the 'crest-jewel of educational institutions'. It is said to have been founded in the fifth or sixth century B.C.

It came into prominence as a centre of learning during the period of the Gupta rulers who, though, orthodox Hindus, contributed a 'lion' share to the development, equipment and endowment. King Kumar Gupta I (414-455 A.D.), Narasimha Gupta (468-472 A.D.) and Buddha Gupta (475-500 A.D.) were the great patrons of Nalanda University.

Early History of Nalanda

According to Hieun Tsang, the renowned Chinese pilgrim of Pilgrims, Nalanda derives its name from the previous birth of Mahatma Buddha. Buddha in one of his previous births on Boddhisattva was a king with his capital at this place. His liberality won for him and his capital the name Nalanda or 'charity'.

According to tradition the place owes its name to a '*Naga*' of the same name who resided in a local tank. Mahavir Swami is said to have spent fourteen rainy season here.

It is said that in course of his journey, Buddha often stayed at this place.

Nalanda is the place of the birth and death of Sariputta, the right hand disciple of Buddha.

Emperor Ashoka (third century B.C.) is regarded as the founder of 'Nalanda Vihar'.

Nagarjuna, the famous Mahayan philosopher and alchemist studied here in the second century B.C.

King Harsha (606 to 647 A.D.) gave liberal grants to monasteries at Nalanda and also to University of Nalanda.

Nalanda was located at about 90 km. south of Patna and 11 km. north of Rajgir.

Buildings: Excavations have shown that Nalanda University covered an area of about 1.6 km. long and nearly 3/4 km. broad. The Central Cottage had seven hills attached to it. Besides there were 300 smaller lecture rooms. The buildings were superb several storeys in height.

The entire place was surrounded by an encircling wall.

Number of Students: The Biographer of Yuan Chawang states that in the second quarter of the seventh century the number of students of Nalanda was about 10,000. Students from all parts of India and also from distant foreign countries got admission to the Nalanda University. Yuan Chawang and Itsing were Chinese scholars that were attracted to Nalanda by its fame as centre of learning.

Teachers of Very High Learning and Piety: Yuan Chwang says, 'In the establishment were some thousand brethren, all men of great learning and ability, several hundreds being highly esteemed and famous; the brethren were very strict in observing the precepts and regulations of their order; learning and discussing they found the day too short; day and night they admonished each other, juniors and seniors mutually helping to perfection. Hence foreign students came to the establishment to put an end to their doubts and then became celebrated, and those who 'stole' the name (of Nalanda) were all treated with respect wherever they went. The names of deep scholars and skilful debators, who had distinguished themselves at the University, used to be written in white on the lofty gate of the University for being known to every fresher and visitor.

The head abbots of Nalanda used to be as much celebrated for piety as for scholarship. Amongst them were Dharmapala and Chandrapala, who gave a fragrance to the Buddha's teachings, Gunamati and Sthiramati of excellent reputation among contemporaries, Prabhamitra of clear argument, Jnanamitra of elevated conversation, Jnanamitra of model character and perspicacious intellect and Silabhadra whose perfect excellence was buried in obscurity. These scholars were not, however, content merely to teach and expound; they were authors of several treatises, widely studied and highly valued by their contemporaries. The above seven scholars flourished in the first half of the 7th century; the total number of high class scholars produced at Nalanda during its history of about 700 years must have been very great. At the time of Yuan Chwang's visit the average scholarship of the establishment also was very high.

Rush for Admission from India and Abroad: There was a great rush for admission to the Nalanda University. Students from all parts of India and also from distant foreign countries were anxious to get the benefit of its instructions. Several scholars like Hieun Tsang, Itsing, Ihon-me, Hiuen Chiu, Taou-hi, Hwui-nich, Aryavarman, Buddhadharma, Taou-Sing, Tang and Hwui Lu, from countries like China, Korea, Tibet and Tokhara had spent considerable time at Nalanda. Only two or three out of ten succeeded.

Library Facilities: The Nalanda authorities had realised that a monastery without a library was like a castle without an armoury. The University was maintaining a splendid library to meet the needs of the hundreds of teachers and thousands of students that were engaged in the study of different sciences. One of the reasons why Chinese scholars used to spend months together at Nalanda was to get true copies of the sacred texts and other works of Buddhism. Itsing got copied at Nalanda 400 Sanskrit works amounting to 5,00,000 verses. Significantly enough the library quarter was known as *Dharma-ganja* 'Mart of Religion'. It was located in three splendid buildings appropriately called *Ratna-sagara* (Sea of gems), *Ratnodadhi* (Ocean of gems), *Ratnaranjaka* (Collection of gems).

Curriculum: The curriculum at Nalanda was very comprehensive and catholic. The establishment belonged to the Mahayana school of Buddhism, but the works of the rival school, the Hinayana one, were also taught. This necessitated a study of Pali language, in which most of the Hinayana works were composed. Works of the famous Mahayana scholars like Nagarjuna, Vasubandhu, Asanga and Dharmakirti must have been specially studied. But it is not to be supposed that the curriculum of the University was a sectarian one in the sense that it neglected Hindu subjects. In the first place it must be noted that subjects like grammar, logic and literature were common to both the Hindus and the Buddhists. Secondly, we have to remember that Buddha and Hindu religion and philosophy had become so intricately interconnected with each other that to study the one without the other had become practically impossible not only for the ambitious controversialist but also for the sincere lover of truth. Buddhists themselves inform us that the three Vedas, Vedanta and Samkhya philosophy were taught at the University along with 'miscellaneous works'. The latter expression probably included the study of subjects like Dharmasastra (sacred law), Puranas, astronomy, astrology, etc., which were very important for the lay Hindu and Buddhist students. The study of medicine *chikitsasastra,* which is referred to in the sacred canon, was also prosecuted at the place.

Learning Arrangement: More than fifty subjects were taught. There were about thousand competent teachers to look after the education of about 10000 students. On the average, therefore, each teacher was incharge of about not more than 10 students. Personal attention was given and the teaching was very efficient. Everyday the authorities used to arrange about one hundred lectures. Learned teachers were highly respected as they were experts in the art of teaching.

Methods of Instruction: Methods of instructions included: (i) Verbal, (ii) Explanatory, (iii) Lecture, (iv) Discussion.

Discipline: According to Hieun Tsang, "The students of this university were nothing less than ideal students and since its establishment, there was not a single case of breach of discipline."

Boarding and Lodging Arrangement: Monk students resided in monasteries especially built for the purpose. Monasteries were double storied and had both single seated and double seated rooms. Hearths of huge dimension have been discovered, proving that there were adequate messing arrangements. The University had 200 rich villages as endowment and could therefore offer free boarding and clothing to its students. These facilities were provided to those lay students who agreed to do some menial service.

Administration: At the head of the general administration was the Principal or the Kulpati (Chancellor) who used to be assisted by two Councils, one academic and the other administrative. To arrange for the free boarding and lodging of so vast a number of students was a very costly affair. The University was enabled to do it because different kings had assigned the revenues of a large number of villages for the upkeep of the establishment. The number of these villages was 200 during I-sing's stay at the University (c. 675-685 A.D.).

It is stated that students were involved in managing several type of affairs.

The Destruction of the University: The ruin of the establishment was brought about by the Muslim invaders under Bakhtiyar Khilji towards the beginning of the 13th century. From *Tabakai-i-Naseri*, we learn that the buildings were burnt or destroyed and the whole of the monk population was put to the sword. Thus perished this famous university at the hands of fanatic invaders, who did not know its value.

Summing up: In the words of Dr. R.S. Tripathi, "Its lofty structure, its inspiring instruction imparted through discussion, its comprehensive curriculum, its large assemblage of students from far and near, and above all, the noble character and deep scholarships of its teachers, and alumni were then matters of pride to the entire Buddhist world."

Taxila

An Ancient Educational Institution: Takshasila (Sanskrit), Takkasila (Pali) and Taxila (Greek/Roman) now in Pakistan remained an important seat of higher learning and wisdom for more than 2500 years (till the 11th century A.D.). It was the nursery of the Indian as well as of foreign intellectuals

Radha Kumud Mookerji (1947) called Taxila as "the intellectual capital of the Indian sub-continent".

According to Iqbal Kaul (1987) "For 2500 years and more, it was the greatest seat of higher learning of the ancient world and the fountain head of all arts, humanities and sciences in the India of the yore". (*Hindustan Times*; March 2, 1987)

The city of Taxila is said to have been founded by Bharata and named after his son Taksha (*Ramayana* VII).

The Buddhists hold the city in great reverence for it is closely connected with birth stories of Bodhisattva. It is referred to several times in the majority of the 547 Jatakas.

Taxila has also a special significance for the Jains. Rishaba, the first Tirthankar is said to have visited the place.

Taxila, in the ancient times, was a great hub of world commerce. Three great routes—one from Patliputra to Gandhara, the second from Greece and the third from Central Asia, passed through it.

For over 1500 years, from around 517 B.C. to A.D. 1020, it was ruled by about 30 kings of several races.

In the days of Asoka, the Great Taxila was one of the greatest and most splendid cities of the East.

Takshasila remained buried in the debris of the past decades till 1860 when the excavations made under the supervision of Alexander Cunningham, the first Archaeological Surveyor of India (1860-85), brought to light some facts about the existence of the city. Successive excavation expeditions of John Marshall from 1912 to 1934, uncovered 12 cities of Taxila and numerous shrines. Marshall's findings are found in his book *Guide to Taxila* and the three-volume *monumental dissertation Taxila*.

Chief Features of Taxila University: Dr. Ved Mitra, in his book *Education in Ancient India* (1964) explains the essential features of the Taxila University in these words, "There were no degree examinations, and no degrees or diplomas. In one of the archery schools at Taxila, there were 103 princes on roll from different parts of India. The four Vedas, grammar, philosophy and eighteen 'silpas' or arts were the principal subjects selected for specialisation at Taxila. Among the latter were included medicine, surgery, archery and allied military arts, astronomy, astrology, divination, accountancy, commerce, agriculture, conveyancing, magic, snake-charming, the art of finding treasures, music, dancing and painting". The study of various subjects had a theoretical and a practical course.

Students from distant countries like Korea and China, Burma and Ceylone, Tibet and Nepal used to come to this university "to hear the exposition of obscure metaphysical passages which could be heard nowhere else on earth" as observed by Dr. Ved Mitra.

Teachers of Very High Calibre: Paying tributes to teachers of Taxila, Dr. R.K. Mookerji has observed that the fame of Taxila as a seat of learning was due to its teachers. He states, "They are always spoken of being world-renowned, being authorities, specialists, and experts in the subjects they professed Taxila exercised a kind of intellectual suzerainty over the wide world of letters in India."

Senior pupils helped their teachers in teaching.

According to Iqbal Kaul (March 2, 1987, 'The Hindustan Times'), "Among the famous Taxila alumni were: Physicians Atrey and Jivaka; Prasenajit (later King of Magadha and Buddha's contemporary); grammarian Panini (5th century B.C.), Kautilya (4th century B.C.), Chandragupta Maurya (324-300 B.C.); Physician Charaka, Mahayana Buddhist polyhistor Asvagosha; Mahayana Buddhist Prelate Parvasa, Vasumitra (President of the Fourth Buddhist Council at Kundalvana in Kashmir); Political philosopher Mathara,—all of them flourished at Kanishka's Court (78 A.D. to 101 A.D.); the founder of the Sautantrika School of Himayana Buddhism-Kumaralabdha (3rd century A.D.), pioneer plastic surgeon of the world-sastra (4th century A.D.); the Mahayana Buddhist philosopher brothers—Asanga (4th century A.D.) and Vasubandhu (Samudragupta's Minister); the lexicographer Amarasimha (7th century A.D.) and Surgeon Vagabhatta I (7th century A.D.)."

The Jatakas (5th century B.C.) and the '*Milandapanha*' (2nd century B.C.) provide a detailed exposition of the medical education provided at Taxila.

Admission: The age of admission in all facilities was 16. Taxila University was a great leveller of all distinctions. All students of merit were admitted to the university, irrespective of caste, creed or status. As the *Tila-muthi Jataka* mentions, a student prince Brahmadatta of Kashi, could bring with him only a robe, a pair of one-soled sandals, etc.

Curriculum: The Taxila University imparted instruction on 18 subjects as mentioned in the *'Milandapanaha'*, a Pali Text. The subjects of studies were: arts and crafts, astrology, astronomy, etymology, grammar, interpretation of dreams, omens and signs, itihasa, law, lexicography magic (occult sciences and spells), mathematics, martial arts and sciences, medicine, music, poetry, Indian philosophical thought, Puranas, Vedangas and the Vedas.

The Ramayana (Uttarkanda 101.11) mentions that law was a specialised subject at Taxila.

Among the numerous institutions at Taxila, four were specialised schools—law, medicine, military and political science. The graduates of its various schools were destined to be great scholars and leading lights to play a significant role in the development of Brahmanical and Buddhist learning.

Fees: Students were usually admitted to the university on payment of their entire fee in advance. In lieu of paying the fees in cash, most of the student were allowed to pay in the shape of services to their teachers. Sometimes a student would devote his whole time to studies, without sparing anytime for such services. In such a case the student could pay the fees after the completion of his studies. R.K. Mookerji records "that where students were too poor to be able to pay the teacher's fees in any of the several ways aforesaid a charitable community often came forward to provide for them a free education". State scholarships were also available. Thus it is quite evident that money was no hindrance to higher education.

Residence with the teacher was not compulsory. Day scholars were also admitted.

Valabhi: It was an ancient University, situated in west India at Valabhi, the capital of Maitraka kings during 5th to 8th centuries. It specialised in Hinayana as Nalanda in Mahayana. Like Nalanda, Valabhi attracted students from all parts of India. Once the famous scholars Sthiramati and Gunamati were incharge of the monastery at Valabhi. Besides purely religious studies, the university provided secular studies like Dharma, Niti and Chikitsa (Medicine) Shastras, Accountancy, Economics and Law, etc.

Itsing informs us that its fame rivalled with that of Nalanda in eastern India.

Like Nalanda, Valabhi also provided for Buddhist and Brahmanical studies. Brahmanas from the distant gangetic plains used to send their sons to this seat of learning for higher education. Students from all parts of India used to assemble at Valabhi and stay there for at least two or three years to discuss 'possible and impossible doctrines'. They used to become famous for their wisdom, when they were assured of the correctness of their opinions by the scholars at Valabhi. The names of the famous scholars of the University were written in white on its lofty gates, as was also done at Nalanda.

Financial Support. Valabhi was a rich city. It is said that it had a hundred citizens whose wealth amounted to a million.

The princes also provided considerable support to this university. The Maitraka kings, who were ruling there during c. 480 to 775 A.D., were also great patrons of learning. They used to give direct grants for the purpose of meeting the general expenses of the University as also for strengthening its library. Scholars who completed their educational course at the University used to receive either appointments in government service or some financial help to enable them to start their life. This continued till 775 A.D. when the reigning dynasty succumbed to an Arab attack, which naturally paralysed the work of the University for sometime. The successors of the Maitrakas, though not so well known to history, continued their patronage of the University as soon as the normal times returned, and the place continued to be a famous centre of education attracting students even from distant Bengal down to the 12th century.

Vikramsila University

Vikramsila, founded by King Dharampala in the 8th century A.D., remained a famous centre of learning for more than four centuries. It was located on a suitable site, a hillock on the bank of the Ganges in northern Magadha. The successors of King Dharampala continued to patronise this university which acquired an international fame.

The Head or the Chancellor of this University was very carefully selected on the basis of his high scholarship and probity of conduct. A Board of eminent teachers controlled the teaching work. It is also stated that the Board also administered the affairs of Nalanda. There were several committees to look after different jobs. Among the important Committees were: Coordination Committee, distribution of food and fuel, and assignment of monastic work etc.

The University had six colleges, each with a strength of 108 teachers.

In the 12th century A.D. there were about 3,000 students in the University.

The University maintained a huge and precious collection of books.

Grammar, Logic, Metaphysics, Tantras and Ritualism were the main subjects studied here.

Although the curriculum was not so extensive as at Nalanda but it was more systematically organised.

This University was probably the only university which awarded degrees and diplomas.

To get admission into the university, the new entrant had to pass an admission test.

Students from Tibet kept coming here for higher education for about four hundred years. Deepankar, the famous scholar of this university went to Tibet for the promotion of learning, culture and religion.

The Tibetan accounts provide a treasure house of information about its scholars.

In 1203, the Vikramsila University was completely destroyed and the library consigned to flame by a Muslim invader Bakhtyar Khilji. Shribhadra, the Chief Protector fled to the University of Jagaddala from where he proceeded to Tibet and settled there. Thus ended this important centre of higher learning.

(*Source*: A.S. Altekar. *Education in Ancient India*, 1957)

OVERVIEW OF ANCIENT INDIAN EDUCATION SYSTEM

Achievement of Ancient System of Education

Educational institutions and especially institutions of higher learning provided a stimulating and vibrant intellectual environment. The educational system was by and large successful in developing character and personality, preservation and enrichment of culture. The system developed sense of self-confidence, self-respect and self-restraint. It fostered powers of discrimination and judgments. It laid emphasis on social obligations. It led to the production of literature of a very high quality. It brought about a remarkable cultural unity. It helped in the spread of learning in several countries of Asia. As observed by Altekar, "The success of Indian missionaries in spreading Hindu and Buddhist culture in South-East, Eastern and Central Asia must be attributed to the success of the educational system in enkindling a strong zest in the minds of the students for spreading national culture far and wide. Above all, the educational system produced independent minds and creative intellects; there is hardly any other civilisation in the world, which went on awakening rich and diverse contributions to the different branches of knowledge for a long and continuous period of two thousand years."

There is no exaggeration in the statement that in ancient times on account of its contribution to learning and education including scientific and secular literature, India was called '*Jagat Guru*' (World Teacher). India enjoyed fame for thousands of years in countries like China, Central Asia, Korea, Java, Siam, Sumatra and Tibet, etc.

Following were the merits of the educational system.

1. *Stress on Duty*: The entire educational system was geared to develop a sense of duty towards oneself and others.
2. *Balanced Approach to the Ideals of Liberation and Worldly Affairs*: While stressing the ideal of life as '*Mukti*' (liberation) or oneness with the divine, the system of education did not neglect professional and vocational pursuits.
3. *All Round Development*: Stress was laid on aesthetic, cultural, physical, religious and spiritual development.
4. *Education in Natural Surroundings*: Educational institutions were located in the lap of nature.
5. *Teacher-Pupil Contact*: There was an intimate contact between the teacher and the taught.
6. *Gurukul System*: Residential educational institutions provided the homely as well as appropriate educational environment.
7. *Well-Regulated Life of the Students*: While living in the hermitage (*Ashram*) of the teacher, the students lived a well-regulated and well-disciplined life.
8. *Training for Citizenship and Social Life*: Ancient education by providing a corporate life, trained the students in the 'Art of Living' which implied the development of qualities of citizenship and social life. 'Self sacrifice' aspect was always stressed.
9. *Specialised Education*: There was enormous scope for specialising in a particular branch of discipline. The

Temple Colleges of the South and the Institutes of higher learning in other parts of India (Universities) provided a variety of disciplines with specialised teachers.

10. *Women's Education*: Education of women was given its due attention. In the Vedas, several hymns are attributed to learned women.
11. *No State Interference*: Although the State patronaged educational institutions with endowments, yet it did not interfere in the functioning of institutions.
12. *Education of the Masses*: Education was freely available to all sections of population.
13. *Advancement in Medical Science*: India enjoyed a high reputation in the field of medical science. Indian physicians were invited to several countries.
14. *Development of Literature*: Ancient India produced great scholars who wrote intensively as well as extensively on philosophy, religion, science and different arts. They went to foreign lands to promote learning.
15. *Free Education*: In general, it can be said that education was free. Students were expected to pay *'Guru Dakshina'* after completing their studies.

Shortcomings and Limitations of the System of Education in Ancient India

When we take into account the ancient system of edcuation in the context of present scenario, following shortcomings and limitations are observed.

1. *Overemphasis on Religious Rituals*: In the field of education several religious ceremonies were performed which had little relevance to the content and methodology of teaching.
2. *Unbalanced Approach*: With the passage of time, education tended to become religion and secular subjects began to be neglected.

3. *Education of the Other World:* It is generally argued that the ancient system of education neglected the present worldly pursuits and laid stress on the other world.
4. *Neglect of Reasoning Aspect*: Too much faith was put on the '*Shastras*'. This made the profile of blind followers. The power of logical thinking was blunted.
5. *Less Emphasis on Vocational Education*: An individual who was well-versed in the scriptures received more importance and manual labour was despised.
6. *Neglect of Military Science*: Under the influence of Buddhist philosophy of non-violence, military science was neglected. There is therefore no wonder, that less than 20 horsemen of a Muslim General could capture Bengal in the medieval period.

Summing up: Notwithstanding some limitations, the system of education in ancient India made its name even in various foreign lands.

5

Education in Medieval Period

With Emphasis on Muslim Education

INTRODUCTION

The period under review covers the system of education in India from about the 10th century A.D. to the middle of the 18th century, i.e., before the British rule.

Educational system discussed in this chapter covers both the Muslim System of Education as well as the Hindu System of Education. It is true that during this period, Muslim System of Education was the predominant system. All the same, there existed Hindu System of Education also which cannot be ignored while discussing Medieval System of Education.

CHIEF CHARACTERISTICS OF MUSLIM EDUCATION

The chief characteristics of Muslim education in India are given here in brief:

1. *Aims of Education*: Following were the main aims of Muslim Education in India:
   (i) Developing love for Muslim culture and religion.
   (ii) Enabling the individual for Islamic life.
   (iii) Preparing the students for the next world, i.e., achieving salvation.
   (iv) Equipping the students for a vocation.

(v) Preparing individuals for running administration.

(vi) Preparing persons for high posts and especially for the interpretation of Islamic law.

2. *Patronage of the Rulers*: The rulers helped in the spread of education. They built educational institutions and universities. They endowed them with funds. Big landlords also provided financial help for the spread of education. The rulers patronised the men of learning.
3. *No State Control on Education*: The rules neither claimed any authority over the educational institutions nor interfered with their management.
4. *Religion Dominated Education.* In the words of S.N. Mukerji, "The whole educational system was saturated with religious ideals which influenced the aim, the contents of study, and even the daily life of the pupils." The pupils acquired knowledge as a religious obligation.
5. *Countryside as the Centre of Education*: By and large, educational institutions flourished in the countryside.
6. *Provision of Various Disciplines:* Though education was primarily religion-oriented, it included the study of many intellectual activities like mathematics, astronomy, grammar, polity and politics. Art and literature were also encouraged.
7. *Norms of Conduct*: Adequate stress was laid on well-defined norms of behaviour, pattern of thought, building up personality and character of the pupils.
8. *Learned Teachers*: Teachers took to teaching for love of learning. They were held in high esteem. Prof. S.N. Mukerji has observed, "Learning was prized for its own sake and as a mark of the highest human development and teaching was never handicapped by examination requirements.
9. *Teacher-Pupil Relationship*: In the Muslim period also the teacher was respected as during the Brahmanic or

Buddhist period. There was intimate relationship between the teacher and the pupil, although the practice of living with the teacher was not as common with the Muslims as it was in the case of Brahmanic and Buddhist period. Pupils were expected to serve the teacher and in return got sometimes free food and always free knowledge from him.

10. *Individualised Instruction*: Since the number of students with the teacher was limited, he paid individual attention to each students.
11. *Monitorial System*. Although a teacher did not have many pupils to teach yet, still the teacher would take the help of senior and advanced students to teach the younger or the junior.
12. *Discipline*, Punishments were quite severe. Truants and delinquents were caned on their palms and slapped on their faces. A strange mode of punishment was to make the children hold their ears by taking their hands from under their thighs while sitting on their tiptoes. Whipping was also quite common. Any form of punishment devised and thought of by the ingenuity of the teacher was permissible.
13. *Types of Institutions*: Primary education, was imparted in *'Maktabs'* and Secondary and High education in *'Madrasahs'*.
14. *Vocational Education*: Provision was also made for vocational, technical and professional education. Professor Weber says, "The skill of the Indians in the production of delicate woven fabrics, in the mixing of colours, the working of metals and precious stones and in all manner of technical arts ... enjoyed a world wide celebrity. The fine fabrics, the beautiful shawls, the painted wares and the gold and silver ornaments of India are ample proof of the fact that there were arrangements for artistic, vocational and technical education. The presence of so many

> magnificent buildings shows that the art of stone cutting had reached its climax. Feroze Shah Tughlaq maintained a regular department of industries."

Emperor Akbar took considerable interest in education as is evident from the following passage from the *'Ain-i-Akbari'*. The passage makes interesting reading and provides valuable information on the system of instruction, i.e., curriculum, methods of teaching etc.

"In every country, but especially in Hindustan, boys are kept for years at school, where they learn the consonants and vowels. A great portion of the life of the students is wasted by making them read many books. His Majesty orders that every school boy should first learn to write the letters of the Alphabet, and also learn to trace their several forms. He ought to learn the shape and name of each letter, which may be done in two days, when the boy should proceed to write the joined letters. They may be practised for a week, after which the boy should learn some prose and poetry by heart, and then commit to memory some verses to the praise of God, or moral sentences, each written separately. Care is to be taken that he learns to understand everything himself; but the teacher may assist him a little. He ought then for some time to daily practise writing a hemistich or a verse, and will soon acquire a current hand. The teacher ought especially to look after five things : knowledge of the letters; meanings of words; the hemistich; the verse; the former lesson. If this method of teaching be adopted, a boy will learn in a month, or even in a day, what it took others years to understand, so much so that people will be quite astonished. Every boy ought to read books on morals, arithmetic, the notation peculiar to arithmetic, agriculture, mensuration, geometry, astronomy, physiognomy, household matters, the rules of Government, medicine, logic the tabi'i, riyazi, and ilahi sciences, and history; all of which may be gradually acquired.

In studying Sanskrit, students ought to learn the Bayakaran, Niyai, Bedanta, and Patanjal. No one should be allowed to neglect those things which the present time requires.

These regulations shed a new light on schools, and cast a bright lustre over Madrasahs."

CHIEF FEATURES OF PRIMARY AND ELEMENTARY MUSLIM EDUCATION

1. *Institution of Primary Education*: Primary education was imparted through the *'maktabs'* which were attached with mosques or were independent of the mosques. *'Khanquahs'* of the saints also at some places served as centres of education. Several learned men also taught students at their residences.
2. *Financing of the Maktabs*: Most of the Maktabs were either patronised by rulers or had endowments. They depended on the charity of the philanthropists.
3. *Management of the 'Maktabs'*: The *'maktabs'* were run under the guidance of the learned *'Maulavis'* (learned Muslim preceptors). They were supposed to be very pious.
4. *Curriculum*: Curriculum varied from place to place but the teaching of alphabets and the recitation of the Quran was almost compulsory. The students learnt some portions of Quran by heart as this was considered essential to perform religious functions.
5. *Languages*: Arabic and Persian languages were mostly compulsory. For getting high government posts, one had to learn these languages.
6. *Fees*: There were several village schools where the students were required to pay for their instruction, not in cash but in kind.
7. *Orphanages*: The state set up some orphanages where the children received education free of charge. Vast

endowments were made for these orphanages.

8. *Age of Admission*. At the age of four years, four months and four days, '*Maktab*' ceremony or '*Bismillah*' was performed to indicate the beginning of education of the child. This was considered as an auspicious moment for initiation or starting education. Good wishes were offered to the child. '*Surah-i-Iqra*' a chapter from the holy Quran was recited on this occasion.
9. *Education of the Sons of Nobles and Rulers*: The Muslim nobles as well as rulers engaged tutors to teach their children at home.
10. '*Wide-spread Maktabs*': Almost every village had at least, one '*Maktab*'. There were several '*Maktabs*' in towns and cities.
11. *Curriculum and Mode of Instruction*:
    (i) During those days there were no printed books for the beginners. Wooden boards (*taktis*) were used for writing letters of the alphabet. Dust was also used for this purpose.

    (ii) *The Quran*: After alphabets, words were taught to students. The teacher dictated these words from the Quran.

    Memorisation was insisted upon. The students normally did not understand the meaning.

    (iii) *Stress on Calligraphy*: Beautiful and fine handwriting was an important element of instruction. The teacher demonstrated the mode of writing and the students were asked to imitate the same.

    (iv) *Teaching of Grammar*: Grammar was taught as it was considered very valuable in teaching the languages.

    (v) *Religious Instruction*: Instruction imparted in the '*Maktabs*' was religious through and through.

    (vi) *Books other than Quran*: After the Quran, the

'*Gulistan*' and the '*Bostan*' poems of poet Firdausi were taken up. At some places Persian books like, '*Karima*' by Scholar Sadi and '*Pandnama*' by Attar were studied.

(vii) '*Paharas*': Students also learned '*Paharas*' (multiple of numbers). Students memorised these while uttering collectively in a loud voice.

12. *Buildings*: In general, the students sat on the ground in rows under the shade of a tree and the teacher used mat or dear-skin to sit at. He also attended to the students while standing.

DEVELOPMENT OF MUSLIM EDUCATION DURING THE RULE OF VARIOUS DYNASTIES AND RULERS

Introduction: The Muslim rulers patronised learning and scholars. They gave liberal grants to educational institutions, stipends to students and bestowed several favours in cash and kind to scholars. They gave them suitable jobs also. Nevertheless their interference in the running of educational institutions was almost nil.

In this section, a brief description of the work done by individual rulers as well as dynasties is given.

Mohammad Ghori is reported to have built mosques and colleges. He gave his slaves good education. Qutubuddin was a man of literary tastes and built many mosques which were centres not only of religious worship but also of education. Iltutmash is said to have built a Madrasa and a college existed at Delhi during the reign of Razia.

Nasir-ud-din Mahmud was himself a scholar and he rewarded scholars. At Jalandhar, a college was established during his reign.

During Balban's reign many literary societies are said to have flourished.

Under the Khilji dynasty, Ala-u-din built a Madrashah at Hauz Khas, Delhi, which had become a great centre of learning. Mohammad Tughlaq is said to be a man of great learning and he gave great help and encouragement to scholars. The Mohammadan historian Farishta says that Feroze Shah Tughlaq built no less than thirty colleges with mosques attached.

Lodhis founded many schools and colleges and made education compulsory for military officers.

The best attention given to education was under the Mughals. Babar was a man of great accomplishments, with a knowledge of Arabic Persian and Turkish and a taste for Poetry. A college was built by Humayun at Delhi and by Sher Shah at Narnaul.

Akbar though unlettered was deeply interested in spreading education and learning. He was particularly zealous in building up a great library. He was a patron not only of Mohammadan learning but also of Hindu learning and had a large number of Sanskrit and other books translated into Persian.

Agra, Lahore and Fatehpur Sikri became great centres of literary activities. Numerous Maktabs and Madrasahs were founded and richly endowed. Akbar was not only concerned with the multiplication of Maktabs and Madrasahs but he also wanted that the quality and content of education should be improved. During his reign the curriculum was modified to enable the students to acquire education according to their particular aims and ambitions. None was allowed to neglect those things which the time required.

According to *Ain-i-Akbari* "every boy ought to read books or novels, arithmetic, agriculture, mensuration, geometry, astronomy, household methods, the rules of government, medicine, logic, the physical sciences and history."

(Details are given earlier)

Akbar said, "Care was to be taken that he (the pupil) learns to understand everything himself but the teacher may assist him a little." It may be observed that he advocated self-study with a proper guidance by the teacher. The curriculum advocated by Akbar shows that the subjects of practical utility were not neglected. His main emphasis was on the teaching of morals. The work of Akbar was in no way undone by his successor—Jahangir and Shah Jahan. All the educational institutions with their rich endowments continued in unabated prosperity.

Aurangzeb was himself well versed in Arabic, Persian, his mother-tongue, Chughtai, Turkish, in several arts and sciences, in theology and Arabic Grammar. He founded many schools and colleges. Imperial Firmans were issued to Provincial Governments to look to the education of their subjects. But his attitude towards Hindu educational institution was not fair. It is said that in 1669 he ordered many Hindu schools and temples to be destroyed though other Muslim rulers had tolerated them.

Aurangzeb however had very progressive views on education. To him the prevailing methods and content of education were utterly useless. About the education of princes, for example, he wanted that they should be "acquainted with the distinguishing features of every nation of the earth, its resources and strength; its mode of warfare, its manners, religious form of government". According to him, "origin of states, their progress and decline" must be studied. He considered the subject of history as a most vital study for princes. He hated verbalism and wasting too much time on grammar, language and law. Comprehensive knowledge elevating the individual and rendering him of glorious deeds was his ideal. He preferred sciences to philosophy. He wanted the study of philosophy to train the intellect for reasoning power, instead of stuffing the intellect with foolish propositions. To him mother tongue, rather than Arabic, was a convenient medium of instruction.

Summing Up

Mohammadan learning in India like the medieval learning of Europe had become formal and scholastic, with a strong emphasis on grammar. But it may be said that History was a very favourite subject in the Muslim period but as expected it did not activise scientific and critical attitude of the present.

'THE MADRASAHS' OR 'MADRASAS'

Main features of Education in 'Madrasahs' and of Higher Education and Learning

Meaning: The *'Madrasahs'* imparted secondary and higher education. Often these Madrasahs were attached to mosques. The term *'Madrasahs'* is derived from Arabic word *'dars'* (a lecture) and means a place where lecture is given. There was difference in principle between the Madrasa and other mosques. When a particular room was set apart in a mosque for the teaching purposes it was called a Madrasah. Sometimes it was quite close to a large mosque. It functioned as college of higher education where eminent scholars taught different subjects by using the lecture method supplemented by discussions. Management was usually private supported by state grants and endowments. The content of the curriculum was both religious and secular and covered a period from 10 to 12 years. Religious education comprised deep study of the Quran, Islamic law and Sufism. Literature, logic, history, geography, astronomy, astrology, arithmetic, agriculture and medicine were the secular subjects taught in Madrasa. Some Madrasas had hostels attached to them which provided free boarding and lodging.

I. *Curriculum*: Prof. Krishan Lal Ray in his book *'Education in Medieval India* (1984) observes, "We do not get any definite information as to the curriculum followed in the *'Madrasahs'*.

1. Prof. Ray refers to a publication entitled *'Khulasatu-i-Maktib* (1688 A.D.) which contains a detailed list of the Persian texts used in *'Madrasahs'*. According to it, a set curriculum from the time of Iltutmash was followed. It was mainly theological. The main subjects taught in the *'Madrasahs'* were: *'Tasfiz'* (*Quranic* Exigencies), *'Hadis'* (Traditions of the Prophet), and *'Fiqh'* (Muslim Jurisprudence). Besides, grammar, literature, logic, mysticism and scholasticism were taught.
2. According to Badaoni, a historian of Akbar's time, curriculum was divided with two groups, namely Science and Non-science. Science group included subjects that required the use of intellect. Subjects under these were: astronomy, arithmetic, astrology, mechanics and philosophy. Other subjects required the exercise of memory.
3. Abul Fazal in *'Ain-i-Akbari'* mentions three types of subjects as under:
   (a) *'Ilahi'* : This included theology or divine science.
   (b) *'Riyazi'* : It comprised astronomy, medicine, mathematics and music.
   (c) *'Tabiqi'* : It included all physical sciences during Aurangzeb's time, the curriculum included these subjects : *'Tasfiz'* (Quranic exigencies), *'Fiqh'* (Muslim gurisprudence), *'Hadis'* (Traditions of the Prophet), grammar, logic, mathematics, philosophy, rhetoric and syntax.
4. In the theology-based curriculum of higher education among the Muslims, Akbar introduced several reforms and introduced secular orientation to curriculum. He laid down the principle that every boy ought to read books on the following subjects:
   (i) Agriculture
   (ii) Arithmetic

(iii) Astronomy
(iv) Geometry
(v) Household matters
(vi) History
(vii) Mensuration
(viii) Medicine
(ix) Logic
(x) Rules of Government
(xi) *'Tabiq'* (Physical Science)
(xii) *'Riyazi'* (Science that relates to quantity)
(xiii) Science

The knowledge of these subjects was graded and was to be gradually acquired.

In the schools meant for Sanskrit learning, *'Vyakarna'* (Grammar), *'Nyaya'* (Logic) and Patanjali's commentary were taught.

The Hindu students were admitted in *'Maktabs'* and *'Madrasahs'* and sometimes they excelled the Muslim students.

Humayun took a great interest in astronomy. Akbar issued an order that students must learn medicine. Both Ayurvedic and Unani system of medicine were taught side by side.

5. Prof. M. Akhtar Siddiqui, in an article published in the *'University News'* (July 29, 1996), under the caption 'Revitalising Madrasa Education', refers to an unpublished Ph.D. Dissertation of Ahmad (1990). The development of curriculum in the Madrasas can be divided into the four periods as given below:
   (i) In the first period ranging between 7th and 8th century *'Hijra'* (13th and 14th century A.D.), great emphasis was laid on *Sarf-O Nahu, Balaghat, Fiqh, Usule Fiqh, Mantiq, Kalam, Tasawwuf* and *Tafseer*. In this period little emphasis was laid on Hadith.

(ii) In the second phase starting from 9th century Hijra (15th century A.D.), greater attention was paid to the teaching of *Hadith*.

(iii) In the third phase of curriculum like Physiology, Physics and Mathematics, besides *Hadith* were also included in the curriculum.

(iv) The fourth phase of development of Madrasa curriculum in the country led by Mulla Nizamuddin gave birth to *Darse-Nizami* or Nizamuddin System which was introduced in the early eighteenth century A.D. Modern subjects like Mathematics, Algebra, Astronomy, Physics and Physiology began to be emphasised.

6. The curriculum drawn by Mulla Nizamuddin in the 18th century included the following subjects.
   (i) Declination and Conjugation
   (ii) '*Hadis*' (Traditions of the Prophet)
   (iii) '*Tasfiz*' (Quranic Exigencies)
   (iv) '*Fiqh*' (Muslim Jurisprudence)
   (v) Dialectics
   (vi) Grammar and Syntax
   (vii) Mathematics
   (viii) Logic
   (ix) Philosophy
   (x) Rhetoric
   (xi) Principles of Jurisprudence

II. *Medium of Instruction*: In Muslim educational institutions, instruction was imparted through the medium of Persian.

III. *Development of Urdu*: During the course of time, on account of the mixing of the Muslims with the Hindus, a new language, namely Urdu, emerged. It became the common language of conversation in Northern India.

IV. *Method of Instruction*: Learning book by rote as well as through the prescribed books was in vogue. In the beginning of the Muslim rule, teaching was mostly oral probably for want of convenient material. Emperor Akbar introduced writing of the alphabet first for effective teaching. Discussions and seminars were also held for a better comprehension and understanding of the subject-matter.

V. *Residential 'Madrasahs'*: In general, the *'Madrasahs'* were residential. However, day scholars were also admitted at some places.

VI. *Relation between the Teacher and the Students*: There were close and cordial relations between the teachers and the students.

VII. *Assessment*: Assessment by the teacher was final.

VIII. *Degrees*: (i) The degree of *'Fazil'* was awarded to a student who specialised in logic and philosophy, (ii) The degree of *'Alim'* was awarded to those who specialised in the theology, (iii) *'abil'*. Those who specialised in literature, received the degree of *'abil'*. Degrees were awarded at a ceremony.

IX. *Status of Teachers*: Teaching profession was considered a dignified profession and teachers were highly respected.

X. *Monitorial System*: The monitorial system was in vogue.

XI. *Types of Institution*: Most of the educational institutions were funded and run by private individuals. There were also state-aided and state sponsored educational institutions. Huge endowments were made to the educational institutions for their maintenance.

XII. *Technical and Vocational Education*: Technical education was encouraged by several Muslim rulers like Ala-u-din Khilji, Firoz Shah Tughlaq and Sher Shah. Akbar and Jehangir took special interest in the promotion of technical education.

XIV. *Fees*: Fees were not charged from the students who rendered personal service in those institutions which were held in private homes.

CENTRES OF LEARNING OF MUSLIM EDUCATION

Agra: Agra became a radiant centre of Islamic culture and philosophy. Many Madrasahs were established here by Sikandar Lodhi, Babar and Humayun. But it was Akbar who made Agra not only a centre of learning and education but also a centre of culture and fine arts. Jahangir, Shah Jahan and Aurangzeb added many Madrasahs and educational institutions and gave financial help. Jaffar in his book entitled, "*Muslim Education in India*" has observed, "Men of learning and erudition from Arabia, Persia and Bokhara found patronage from the rulers of India, who were remarkable for their munificence ... The result was that in course of time Agra grew into a great literary city, containing several schools and colleges where people flocked from far and wide for higher education."

Bidar: It was a very important seat of Islamic education in South India. There was a big Madrasah which contained about 3000 books on Islamic theology, culture, philosophy, medical science, astronomy, history etc. Bahmani rules were very particular about spreading education.

Delhi: The tradition of learning and education was firmly established in Delhi when the Sultanate made Delhi its headquarters. Through their initiative, the Sultans built Madrasah, for example, Il-tutmash was the first to establish a Madrasah at Delhi named *Madarsa-i-Muizzi* after Shahab-ud-din Muhammad Ghouri, Sultana Raziya committed to the charge of Minhaj-i-Siraj, the author of the *Sabaqat-i-Nasri*, the *Nasrai* college. There was also the *Muizzi* College. Amir Khusrau and his spiritual master Nizamud-din Auliya contributed much to the cultural and educational life of Delhi. Literary societies were formed and the most famous which initiated such societies was Khan-i-Shahib (Balban's son and Sayyadi Molla). Mohammed Tughlaq founded a Madrasa in Delhi with a mosque attached to it. Al Qal Qashandi, the author of *Subbu'l A'* says that there were 1000 schools, Madrasas and Maktabs in Delhi in the time of Tughlaq. It is difficult to accept these figures as the precise mode of collection and scrutiny of data had not been devised. Firoz Tughlaq built a college with mosques attached. This Madrasa was situated within the well planted garden and had suitable buildings for the residence of teachers and scholars and the foreign dignitaries used to visit it. Maulana Jalal-ud-din Kirmani was the Principal of this institution. Literary activities and the building of Madrasas and giving endowments continued throughout the period, and almost in every Sultan's rule there was a coterie of scholars and intellectuals, poets and musicians whose recognition by men of authority was a by-word.

During the Mughal period, it was Humayun who built a Madrasa in Delhi in which Sheikh Hussain was the professor, and special provision was made there for teaching mathematics, astronomy and geography.

For long, a college on the roof of Humayun's tomb was used which was at one time an institution of some importance. Shah Jahan founded an Imperial College at Delhi in the vicinity of Jama Masjid, which fell into ruins long before 1857. The Mughal family got a scholar in Dara Shikoh; Abu Talib Kalim was the poet laureate, and Hafiz Muhammad Khiyali was a great 'alim' of his time. Of historical works '*Badshahnama*' of Abdul Hamid Lahori and *Amal-i-Swaleh* may be mentioned. Shah Jahan opened the college *Dar-ul-Baqa* (abode of eternity) with Maulana Sadrud-din as its Director. The Madrasah at Roshan-ud-daulah in Delhi owed its existence to private efforts and munificence. Aurangzeb's theory of education is embodied in the reproach that he administered to his teacher Mullah Sale who concentrated on the rules of grammar but failed to impart to him liberal education. Aurangzeb complained to his teacher that the kind of instruction imparted to him was destitute of natural philosophy, rationalism, geography, and was confined to linguistic studies which 'ruin the mind and fatigue the soul'.

The accounts of British officials on education show that still quite a number of educational institutions managed to exist, though in the enumeration of these schools there appears obviously a wide divergence in different accounts. The report of 1827 gives for the Southern division of Delhi 27 Muslim schools with 209 pupils and 24 teachers. Another report dated 15th June 1827, which Charles Matcalfe received, gives details of 31 schools in the district of Delhi with 247 Hindu scholars and 116 Muslim scholars. Again Matcalfe's statement of the number of native schools situated in Delhi and its vicinity (dated 15th June 1827) shows that there were 147 schools in Delhi, 40 of which were Hindu schools and 103 Persian schools. The monthly salary of a teacher varied between Rs. 3/- to Rs. 9/-. I.H. Taylor's account of 8th January, 1824 states that the number of public seminars and colleges under the management of local agents was 17 and number of scholars 81, whereas the number of private seminars and colleges in Delhi was 17 and that of scholars 184. The account derived from the Friend of India (1818) shows that there were 30 Persian schools and 45 Arabic schools in the city of Delhi. The Sanskrit schools numbered 20, and the Hindi schools were as many as 41. The number of scholars studying in these schools was unequal ranging between 5 to 50.

The well known public and private schools were the Madrasas attached to Kashmire Masjid, which was going to decay for want of funds, the Madrasa of Nawab Rosoan-ud-Dowlah, Fatehpuri Masjid Madrasa, Masjid Kotwal Chabutra and Masjid Mori Gate Madrasa.

Jaunpur: It was once a great seat of Muslim learning. In the time of Sultan Ibrahim Sharqui (1401-1440) it was the capital of the kingdom of Jaunpur where hundreds of Madrasas and Masjids lay scattered and where teachers and scholars were granted lands and endowments so that they might completely devote to learning. Firoz Tughlaq fixed liberal stipends to the learned men and teachers of Jaunpur, but Sikander Lodhi after his conquest of Jaunpur ordered the destruction of important buildings including the Madrasas. During the reign of Mughal emperors it again enjoyed its high reputation. State reporter stationed at Jaunpur had to send regular reports about the progress of every Madrasa, and fresh grants were sanctioned as and when required.

Malwa: It was a great centre of Muslim learning under the patronage of Sultan Mahmud Khilji about the middle of the 15th century. According to Farishta, it could bear a fair comparison with Shiraz or Samarkand in literary excellence. It rose to be a great resort of distinguished philosophers and literary men who came not only from the different parts of the kingdom of Malwa but also from other countries.

A CRITIQUE OF MUSLIM EDUCATION

A. Merits of Muslim Education

1. *Emphasis on Education*: Education was considered as an instrument of procuring happiness in this world and obtaining knowledge of god. Knowledge was considered as a source of solutions of all the religious problems. The prophet Muhammad has said, "To seek knowledge is a duty for every Muslim". Education was considered as a remover of barrier between an individual and God.
2. *Personal Contact between the Teacher and the Taught*: The teacher showed immense love and affection to the students and the students immense respect and reverence to the teacher.
3. *Individual Attention*: Since the number of students under the charge of a teacher was quite reasonable, it was easy to pay individual attention to their optimum development and progress.
4. *Vocational Aspect*: Notwithstanding stress on religious education, the system of education was planned in a

manner that students were prepared for vocational pursuits also.

5. *Inclusion of Secular Education*: A large number of secular subjects like astronomy, agriculture, commerce, handicrafts and medicine etc. were included in the curriculum.
6. *Development of Historical Literature*: The Muslim rulers patronised scholars who wrote valuable books (*Memoirs*) etc. like biographies which throw a lot of light on everyday life including education. The rulers themselves wrote their '*Memoirs*'.
7. *Free Education*: Students were not required to pay any fee. These was also free boarding and lodging.
8. *Natural Surroundings*: '*Madrasahs*' were normally located in natural environment. The students could enjoy the bounties of nature as well as pursue their studies.

Limitations and Shortcomings of Muslim Education

1. *Mother-Tongue not the Medium of Instruction*: Persian and Arabic were the medium of instruction. The foreign medium put heavy strain on the learners.
2. *Very Little Check on Standards*: In the absence of any external evaluation, it was not possible to compare the quality of education imparted in one institution with the others.
3. *Much Emphasis on Religious Scriptures*: Secular subjects were neglected at the cost of religious scriptures.
4. *Less Facilities for Higher Education*: '*Madrasah*' were usually located in big towns and cities. It was, therefore, very difficult for the rural people and people residing at small places to avail of the opportunity of higher education.
5. *Defective Method of Teaching, Writing and Reading*: The student was first required to practise the reading of words and after acquainting with this, he was taught to

write. This involved wastage of time.

6. *Neglect of Women Education*: It is true that royal ladies were able to receive education but in general women education was neglected.
7. *Cramming*: There was over-emphasis on cramming and less on comprehension and understanding.

6

Hindu System of Education During the Medieval Period

INTRODUCTION

With political changes, radical changes in various forms in different areas are bound to come in a country. They become all the more pronounced when some foreign power holds its sway. This happened in the case of India also. The Muslims rulers, who came from outside, had an altogether different culture, a different philosophy, a different religion and a different language. The intermingling of different cultures, religions, philosophies, etc. produces major changes. This also had its impact on education in varying degrees.

CHIEF FEATURES OF HINDU SYSTEM OF EDUCATION IN INDIA DURING THE MEDIEVAL PERIOD

1. *Lack of State Support*: With the advent of the Muslim rule, the state support for the Hindu system of education almost ended. Now it depended upon the rich people, scholars and village communities. Of course where there were no Muslim rulers, it received state support. Gradually there remained a few such areas.
2. *Religion Oriented Education*: The system of education, by and large was dominated by religion.

3. *The 'Pathshalas'*: Elementary education was imparted in '*Pathshalas*' which existed both in villages and towns.
4. *Building of 'Pathshalas'*: Usually '*Pathshalas*' were held in the verandah of some house or under trees. There were also separate houses for '*Pathshalas*'. Specific type of buildings for them did not exist. Premises of the temples were also used.
5. *Fees*: No regular fees were charged from the students. The parents gave presents to the teachers. Students were required to render personal service to the teachers. Sometimes teachers also engaged themselves in part time work to supplement their income.
6. *Instructional Methods at the Elementary Stage*: There were four stages of instruction at the elementary stage.

   In the first stage writing letters of the alphabet on sand was taught to students.

   In the second stage, the teacher wrote on palm leaves and the students traced over them with red pen and charcoal ink. These cold be rubbed very easily.

   In the third stage, the student wrote and pronounced compound components. Excessive practice was given to the students in this regard. Common names of persons were used for this purpose. At this stage also, the student was taught to use the words in the formation of sentences. He was also taught to make a distinction between written and colloquial languages.

   The students were taught the rules of arithmetic and multiplication tables repeated by the entire class.

   In the fourth stage, students were taught to use paper for writing.
7. *Curriculum at the Elementary Stage*:

   (i) Knowledge of weights and measures was considered essential. Therefore, arithmetic was a compulsory subject at the elementary stage. According to Dr.

Krishnalal Ray, (1989), the elementary schools were mainly for giving instruction to these R's and then practical application (such as composition of letters and business documents).

(ii) Literature was included in the curriculum, real literary taste was not cultivated.

(iii) Moral and religious instruction also had a secondary place in these schools.

(iv) In some schools, salutation to Goddess Saraswati (the Goddess of Learning) was learnt by heart by the students.

(v) Instruction in mythology and sacred love of the Hindus was also given in some schools.

HINDU HIGHER EDUCATION INSTITUTES IN MEDIEVAL INDIA

It was really very unfortunate that some of the best institutes of higher learning of the Hindus were destroyed by Muslim conquerors. The most notable example is that of Nalanda — an international centre of learning.

Here description of some of the institutions, which survived, is given.

Kashmir: In the 10th century A.D., with the conquest of Punjab by the Muslims, a large number of scholars from this place migrated to Kashmir. Kashmir remained an important centre of Hindu learning till the last quarter of the 19th century A.D. It is said that a large number of Kashmiri Pandits gave free education to about a dozen students. A large number of Brahmanas lived in this valley and they continued the tradition of Indian learning. There were women scholars also.

Banaras (Kashi/Varanasi/Banaras): According to Abul Fazal (1551-1602), renowned scholar of the Court of the emperor Akbar, the author of monumental work '*Akbar Nama*', Banaras had been a principal centre of Hindu learning from times immemorial. Scholars came to this place from distant place to received education. The teachers lived in different parts of the town. Generally a teacher had nearly half a dozen students. It is of interest to note that Banaras had no education institution comparable to modern school or college. A student usually spent 10 to 12 years with his teacher to receive education. Besides the Vedas and the Purans, astronomy, geography, medicine and philosophy were taught. Immediately after the establishment of the Muslim rule in India, scholars left this place and migrated in large numbers to South India. During Akbar's time, there was considerable change in the situation. Banaras again became a glorious seat of Sanskrit learning in the sixteenth century. Several learned scholars returned and started imparting instruction. Banaras again regained its position as an intellectual centre of Hindu learning and culture. During Aurangzeb's rule, again there was a great setback to this place.

During the medieval period Sant Kabir and Goswami Tulsidas carried on their activities at Kashi.

Raja Jai Singh (1699-1743 A.D.) of Amber established a college at this place for the education of the princes.

Bernier, a famous traveller of the period compared Banaras with Athens of ancient Greece.

Banaras was particularly known for Vedanta, Sanskrit literature and grammar.

Mithila: Mithila, in North Bihar was famous for specialised study in Logic during the Mughal period. It is said that emperor Akbar was so much impressed by the renowned scholar Raghunandandasa Rai that he gave the entire town of Mithila as gift to him. Raghunandandasa in his turn offered this to his '*guru*'. Such was the relationship between a '*Guru*' and the teacher. The local people also patronised the scholars. In the sixteenth century A.D., Mithila was considered as an important centre of religious as well as secular education. During the period of Shah Jahan, Mithila became famous for renowned poets.

Nadia: Nadia seat of learning was founded in 1063 by a Sena King of Bengal. Very shortly its fame spread and scholars from Mithila began to migrate to this place. Nadia achieved prominence in logic although several other subjects were also taught here. Dialectical discussions among students were common here.

There were several institutions of higher learning known as '*tols*'. The '*tol*' buildings were thatched chambers with mud walls. The total number of students in a '*tol*' was nearly 25. Subjects like astronomy, grammar, law, logic and poetry rhetoric etc. were taught Sanskrit, Prakrit, Pali and Bengali were the languages. The '*Bhagwad Gita*', the '*Bhagavata*' and other Hindu scriptures belonging to different sects were also taught at Nadia. Students belonging to all castes were admitted.

Debates Formed an Important Part of Learning

The Nadia School of '*Nyaya*' was known for its excellence in the subject. Raghunath as its first celebrated student defeated the head of Mithila School of Logic. With this, it began to attract scholars from Mithila.

The Nadia seat of learning flourished till the middle of the 19th century. It is estimated that it had about 4,000 students and 600 teachers in 1860.

Temple College at Tiruvorriyur (South India): This temple college was situated in the Chengalpattu district and became famous in the 13th and 14th centuries. It was meant for the study of grammar and was attached to the local Saiviti Temple.

Every important temple in South India had a college attached to it.